Testing for Teaching

Frank Spooncer

HODDER AND STOUGHTON
LONDON SYDNEY AUCKLAND TORONTO

ISBN 0 340 27689 4

Printed in Great Britain for
Hodder and Stoughton Educational,
a division of Hodder and Stoughton Ltd,
Mill Road, Dunton Green, Sevenoaks, Kent
by Richard Clay (The Chaucer Press) Ltd., Bungay, Suffolk.
Typeset by MULTIPLEX medway ltd, Maidstone.

Contents

Acknowledgements

Thanks are due to the following for permission to include material in this book: F.J. Schonell and Oliver and Boyd (74), M.D. Neale and Macmillan (London and Basingstoke) (76,77), Tony Dunsbee and Ward Lock Educational (103), NFER-Nelson (116), Controller of Her Majesty's Stationery Office (120), H.J. Eysenck and Temple Smith (126), Wiltshire County Council Education Department (143), and P.E. Vernon and Methuen & Co (146).

Hodder and Stoughton Educational also thank the following authors for permission to include material: The Godfrey Thomson Unit (31), J.M. Thyne (35), F. Spooncer (42), G.E. Bookbinder (74), V. Southgate (78, 79), D. Young (81), P.D. Pumfrey (86), and W.E.C. Gillham (120).

The examples of test material reproduced in this book are not necessarily shown in their original size.

Preface

This book is entitled *Testing for Teaching* and that conveys exactly its intention. It would be easy to give you lists of tests, explanations of statistical terms and so on, but this, in my opinion, is only part of the story. Each teacher in each school has a different set of testing requirements, and it would be pointless and presumptuous for me to tell teachers which would be their 'best buy' – although that is a question often asked of so-called experts like myself. What I have tried to do is give a framework of basic principles of test construction, selection and interpretation so that, guided by these principles, you can proceed to construct the programme which is most effective for *you*.

Please don't be misled by the term 'testing': this may make you think only of published tests but, as you read, you will see that it is my belief that published tests are only part of the equipment needed for a satisfactory programme. Your observations, your checklists, your intimate and detailed knowledge of your pupils are equally important; you are, in the sense of this book, testing whenever you get effective feedback, by whatever means, on a child's performance, progress and personality.

The present climate of testing is an interesting and important one. There is a triple tension between the requirements of the individual school, those of the local authority, and those of the nation as a whole. Such tensions have recently been clearly evident in America, and no doubt are likely in any country which is not totalitarian in its approach to education.

The first chapter of this book examines this 'contemporary climate'. Please read it – even if you do so after the later chapters. It is very easy to become a little insular in the privacy of one's own school, and not to be aware of the wind of change which may be blowing just outside the windows. The book aims at helping schools to become self-accounting – that is, capable of assessing their effectiveness by a self-chosen repertoire of procedures, supported, but not dominated, by local authority and national programmes. To evade responsibility for this would be to hand over a significant part of the teacher's freedom to the control of outside agencies.

Whilst the material is organised round the British primary system, the principles are applicable in any country where the school and its teachers retain some responsibility for assessment. Chapters 1 to 5 give basic principles of assessment, whether by external or internal means. Chapters 6 to 8 apply these principles to the basic subject areas of literacy and numeracy, again emphasising coordination between external and internal means. Chapter 9 examines the important question of ability, and the last chapter contains suggestions for effective recording and reporting, and includes sections on less obviously measurable areas such as project work, and the personality and behaviour of pupils.

References have been kept to a minimum within the text to allow for a 'smooth read'. At the end of each chapter there are discussion questions, both for individual and group use at staff meetings and conferences. Throughout the book the teacher is referred to as 'she' and the child as 'he'; this is simply for the convenience of style.

The book is based on several years' experience of lecturing on assessment at teachers' centres, so it has been exposed to the critical gaze of the practitioners. In particular Mrs D.V. Spooncer, head teacher of a large primary school in Kent, has kept my feet on the ground whilst my head reached for the clouds.

1

The Contemporary Climate

The balance of control between local and central agencies in education is an important influence on testing programmes. Where central control of the curriculum exists, testing procedures merely monitor outcomes which have been predetermined outside the school. Equally, where a compulsory curriculum is not specified, a central programme of testing can strongly influence what is taught in schools. This chapter traces some important threads in British and American education, and indicates their relevance to the contemporary scene.

Payment by results

In Britain, Robert Lowe implemented his famous *Revised Code* and its associated *Payment by Results* in 1862. The *Code* arose because the Newcastle Commission had been set up to enquire into what measures, if any, were required for the extension of sound and cheap elementary instruction to all classes of the people. The Commission responded by suggesting:

> A searching examination by competent authority of every child in every school to which grants are paid, with the aim of ascertaining whether these indispensable elements of knowledge are thoroughly acquired, and to make the prospects and position of the teacher dependent to a considerable extent on the results of this examination.

The *Code* thus set up 'standards' which prescribed what children working at each level should have achieved, and inspectors visited the schools armed with precise schedules for testing whether they had indeed been reached. This gave such tight control that Lowe was able to say: 'Teachers desiring to criticise the *Code* were as impertinent as chickens wishing to decide the sauce in which they would be cooked'.

This strait-jacket of curriculum and its assessment gradually loosened so that, by 1905, the Board of Education was offering a *Handbook of Suggestions* for teachers, and the period immediately following the Second War could be called the 'Golden Age' of teacher control. But, for economic and other reasons, there has since then undoubtedly been a swing back to the nineteenth century way of thinking. Rhodes Boyson, for instance, wrote in 1973:

> Each school cannot be allowed to 'do its own thing', as head and staff see fit, whilst the children in the area are compelled to attend. There must be either prescribed national standards which all schools seek to achieve, or complete freedom for parents to decide the type of school they wish their children to attend....
>
> In the last resort.... schools have to be accountable to someone. Minimum standards to be attained by all pupils at various ages would mean they were accountable to the State. There could be national standards laid down that all pupils should attain in literacy and numeracy by the age of seven. At eleven, a fixed body of geographical, historical, literary and scientific knowledge could be added to increased literacy and numeracy.....
>
> Such standards should at each age be attainable by all pupils who were not educationally sub-normal or suffering from brain damage. The examinations could be written and externally marked, or checked orally by HMI's..... The once powerful and influential HMI's ensured that schools were of a set standard. Their visits were feared by teachers and heads when a general inspection was announced.

Boyson's nostalgia for the factory system of the nineteenth century is obvious. Though extreme, he was, however, far from alone in his plea for more central control both of curriculum and 'standards'. James Callaghan's speech at Ruskin College in 1976 set into motion the 'great debate' which was followed by a Green Paper, (DES, 1977) *Education in Schools*. Two quotations may highlight the flavour of the Paper:

> There is a need to investigate the part which might be played by a 'protected' or 'core' element of the curriculum common to all schools.

and

> Growing recognition of the need to demonstrate their accountability to the society which they serve requires a coherent and soundly based means of assessment for the education system as a whole, for schools, and for individual pupils.

Armed with these quotations, we can now proceed to examine the following set of questions which are as relevant to education today as they were to Robert Lowe:
– Who is competent to control what is taught, and to examine the results of the teaching?

- What is accountability in education?
- Must every child in every school be tested?
- What are 'these indispensable elements of knowledge'? Must every subject be tested?

Competency and control

In Britain, really tight control of the curriculum and its assessment by means of centrally prescribed objectives and centrally generated testing procedures does not exist. The imposition of such control would imply that teachers were not competent to set their own targets or to measure whether they have been achieved.

Such a situation has occurred in America, where it was reported that, in 1973, 13 states had passed legislation which related teacher tenure to the achievement of performance-based objectives *'which were predetermined by administrators, and merely assessed by evaluators'*. Such a system reduces the status of teachers to that of technicians, carrying out the orders of outsiders, and suggests that 'teaching is too important to be left to the teachers'.

There are, however, signs of a move towards tighter control of both content and assessment in the British scene also. Many teachers will have assisted in providing material for the Review of Local Authority Curricula required by the Department of Education and Science in 1977, which was followed in 1980 by the significantly titled *Framework for the School Curriculum.*

In the field of testing, the Assessment of Performance Unit (APU), which we shall examine later, was set up with the task of assessing and monitoring the achievement of children at school. Lawton suggests that this swing back to central oversight is in part the fault of teachers themselves. He feels that the 'Golden Age' faded because the teaching profession had been given an opportunity to plan a national curriculum, but had not taken full advantage of it, thus leaving the DES with a good excuse to interfere.[1]

British educationalists of the 1980s thus stand at something of a crossroads. On the one hand, they naturally value their professional independence and freedom of judgement in both curriculum and assessment; on the other, there are clear signs that many groups, both popular and political, wish for a closer look into the secret garden of schools and their curricula.

Accountability and education

It is clear from the Newcastle Commission that the idea of accountability, at least in economic terms, has a long history. Its use as a specifically educational term is much more recent. At its simplest, it implies that he who pays the piper calls the tune: society allocates vast sums of money to education, and is therefore entitled to reassurances that the money has been wisely used. Value for money is demanded.

This investment view of accountability suggests an over-easy analogy with the board of directors of a company who are held publicly accountable to the shareholders for their dealings. But if we ask to whom are schools accountable, and for what, it can easily be seen that this financial model is completely inadequate for education. Several main ways in which schools might be held, or might hold themselves, accountable can be distinguished.

Accountability to society

This has two main strands: economic and human. We have already seen that society rightly expects a return for its money – but what is that return to be? Here the analogy with the boardroom vanishes: whilst we might be distinctly put out if we learned that the Head had spent the children's book allowance on a new car, it is not this sort of accounting that is demanded. If schools do make a profit, it is not one which can be stated in financial terms.

Besides allocating funds to schools, society also delegates responsibilities – a major one being the development of children into adults who can enter and make a positive contribution to their society. Thus a nation is quite entitled to ask whether schools are indeed equipping young people with the knowledge, skills and attitudes necessary for life in the modern world. But it does not follow that, because society is entitled to ask these questions, it can necessarily prescribe the way they are answered.

If we pay into a medical scheme, such as BUPA, we have a general expectation that this will help us to stay healthy and that, if we become ill, steps will be taken to help us. But we do not prescribe how the specialist shall diagnose, nor how he shall treat us – it is the doctor who writes the prescription. Thus, we can argue, society may ask the questions but schools must provide the answers in the form of the curriculum.

Society is, of course, composed of individuals; some of these are parents, some are children. Parents have a double investment: they have paid their rates and taxes, and handed their children into the care of the school. At the very least, therefore, they are entitled to reports on progress, and an assurance that the school is helpful to the child. The notion of accountability to an individual pupil is at present less well established. Certainly teachers will feel responsible for their pupils, and thus ask themselves 'Am I doing the right things for them? Are they progressing as they should?'. In this sense, therefore, the teacher is being accountable to herself.

Professional accountability

In its strongest form, professional accountability implies that, whatever external accountability may be required, teachers are themselves perfectly capable of accepting what has been well described as their stewardship of economic and human resources, and of rendering an account of it. The terms of this account will vary with the educational philosophy of the teacher.

Some, who see education more as a process than as a product, as a journey rather than a destination, will reject the idea of accounting in terms of predetermined ends, or as a series of minimal skills to be achieved at prescribed stages of a child's educational career. Others, who see education more directly as the servant of society, may welcome assistance in setting objective standards for their pupils to attain.

Whatever differences there may be in professional orientation, the basic argument is that teachers do have standards, that these standards are worthy of respect, and that teachers, perhaps with outside assistance, are capable of assessing whether those standards have been achieved.

The various accountabilities may be summarised in a diagram, as in Figure 1.1.

The contrast between central and local control, and perhaps between human and economic accountability, can be shown by a comment on the Green Paper itself. In 1979, Marjoram, then head of the APU, said that the Paper 'pointed us towards a system in which the individual progress of every child is properly and regularly assessed by his teachers.... in which classroom, LEA and national assessments are comparable and interrelatable.... In this endeavour, the APU is proud to play its part.' This presents matters in a different way from the quotation on page 2.

Both statements seem to have the same general message – that an adequate testing system must have several layers – but the order of priorities seems markedly different. The official line highlights the importance of the national and central element, whereas Marjoram, in company no doubt with most teachers, begins from the individual child. Two lines of inference are possible from this apparently slight rearrangement. One concerns who is to benefit from education, the other, how that benefit may best be achieved.

The Green Paper appears to suggest that schools are the servant of society, and that the individual can perhaps best be helped by a national

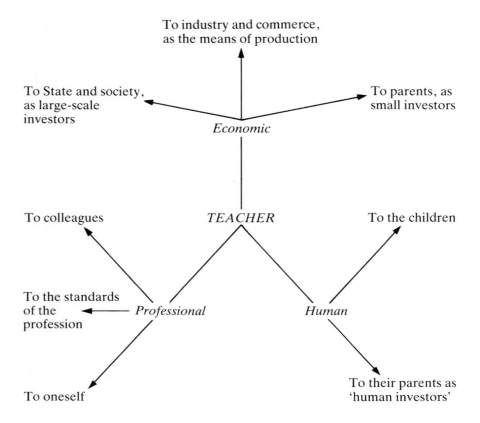

Figure 1.1   What kind of accountability?

system: in other words, if the national scene is well-organised and efficient, the individual pupil must benefit. Marjoram's comment starts from the child, and suggests that only if the foundation of the system – the individual appraisal of individual pupils by individual teachers – is sound can the national system be sound.

Every child? Every subject?

The most extreme opposition to widespread testing of pupils and sub-jects is, of course, to reject any form of testing whatsoever. This strong position is taken by John Holt, (1970), who says:

> I do not think that testing is necessary, or useful, or even excusable. At best, testing does more harm than good: at worst, it hinders, distorts

and corrupts the learning process... our chief concern should not be to improve testing but to eliminate it. How can we expect to measure the content of someone else's mind when it is so difficult, so nearly impossible, to know more than a very small part of the contents of our own?

But this is perhaps a polemic directed more against formal, external tests than against the informal procedures of the classroom teacher. We could, therefore, modify this strong view to one which rejected the imposition of external testing. Thus, a publication of the National Association of Teachers of English claims, more moderately, that 'any teacher with the skill to know his pupils' abilities would not need test materials' (Stibbs, 1979).

The view proposed by this book is that testing, both by external *and* internal means, has value when used appropriately, so that, accepting this view, we can now ask:

– Must we test every child?
– Must we test every subject?
– How often should we test?

Every child

During the 1960s and 1970s, several states in America and some local authorities in Britain instituted blanket surveys, in which every child of a given age (or grade in America) was tested. Such 'every-child' programmes have drawn a number of criticisms:

1. Large-scale programmes may exert considerable backwash effects on the curricula of schools.
2. Unless teachers are closely involved, they take the initiative for testing out of the hands of the school.
3. If the central authority needs a general picture of trends, there is no necessity to test every pupil – smaller samples would suffice.

On the positive side, it can be argued that:

1. The use of the same test throughout any area ensures comparability of standards in that area. This point is very debatable, and is discussed at length in later chapters.
2. They ensure that no child in need of help is omitted by default.
3. They form a means of public accountability for every school in respect of each and every child.

We can look at the pros and cons of these arguments through a medical analogy. It is routine practice to 'nappy-test' all British infants for the presence of phenylketonuria, a metabolic disturbance which can result in deficiency. If it is simply an estimate of what proportion of infants is likely to exhibit the condition, a small, well-chosen sample would be sufficient. But this would not indicate *which* infants were suffering; for that, every-child testing would be needed. Without it some children would escape the net, with drastic consequences.

Thus, we have to find a balance between a programme which is so heavy that it begins to dominate the activities of the school and its pupils, and one which is so vague as to leave gaps in teachers' knowledge of their pupils. The every-child no-child argument is too polarised: we should agree with Marjoram's demand for a multi-layered programme giving different levels of responsibility at different levels of the educational system.

Every subject

It might be argued that to get a true picture of education, whether in a school, an authority or a country, we should assess in every area of the curriculum. If there is to be accountability in one area, why not in another? Again, there are several counter-arguments to this apparently simple suggestion.

1. Some subjects are less amenable to testing than others, indeed some may be destroyed by it. In art, for instance, there is likely to be a greater variation of assessment than in arithmetic. The unfortunate consequence of this could be that we assess only what is easy to assess, and thus increase its importance to the detriment of less objectively measureable areas.

    Creative and expressive subjects are regarded by some as being too sensitive to be tested. The assessment of creative writing against any outside criteria might be thought to be a sure way of inhibiting its spontaneous generation (would you write a poem if you knew it was going to be publicly torn to bits?) and thus a self-defeating exercise.

    This criticism applies most strongly to external measures. Internal measures – the admittedly subjective judgement of teachers – may, of course, be far less obtrusive in their influence. Another sensitive area would be that of moral and personal development, particularly in a multi-cultural society where different beliefs and values are held, quite sincerely, by different groups. Here again, attempts to measure such development might be seen as an affront.

2. Some subjects are more important than others and, therefore, must be assessed. This argument normally centres on the basic skills of numeracy and literacy, some aspects of which prove to be

conveniently easy to test. Again, their importance in a programme of testing might lead to distortion of the curriculum to the detriment of other areas.

3. Minimum competency testing – testing for a prescribed minimal level of achievement – had reached 37 American states by 1980. In many, graduation from high school has been linked to the achievement of a minimal level of competence, defined by the state, usually in the basic skills. The effect of this seems once more to have been preoccupation with the basic skills and a change in the balance of the curriculum. There is, of course, nothing wrong with setting realistic targets for schools and students to achieve, especially when these are likely to be valuable after school. Unfortunately the setting of these minimal targets may lead to the assumption that these are the only true goals of education, and thus to a sad impoverishment of the educational diet.

How often?

In one sense, the teacher is always assessing her pupils. Her daily work inevitably includes this. More formal tests are likely to be intermittent, and their timing and frequency is a matter of some importance. In considering both of these, it may be helpful to introduce some terms concerned with the chronology of testing.

1. *Base-line testing.* At any significant change in a pupil's career – say on transition from infant to junior school – it may be helpful to find what he already knows and can do. This will obviously help in planning his future programme. Similarly, when starting a new topic, teachers will automatically be conducting small base-line assessments – by discussion and questioning for instance – to find how far children have already progressed.

2. *Formative or ongoing testing.* These assessments are made once the educational programme is under way, and again may be formal, as in a half-term test, or informal, as when a teacher walks round her class checking that a new process is understood and correctly applied. Such assessments are formative in that they will shape the next step in the programme, whether for individuals or a group.

3. *Summative testing.* This is literally a summing-up of performance at the end of a significant period of school life. It may summarise what has been achieved in primary school before transition to secondary education, it may be done at the end of a school year, or it may encompass a shorter span, such as what has been learned from a project on weight.

It has several advantages: it can give the teacher information about individual pupils which can be compared with their baseline status to assess progress; it can give the teacher an indication of how far her goals have been achieved and, if pupils are moving on, it can serve as baseline data for the next stage – though holidays are notoriously hard on education!

The dangers of over-frequent testing, particularly when external tests are used, are many. Children may become over-familiar with the tests; they may become test-sophisticated, so that distorted results are obtained. There may be a concentration on what is tested and, as happens in some secondary schools, what is non-examinable may be denigrated. Testing is not a pastime, or a numbers game of attaching a number to a name. Testing, like teaching, should always have a purpose. Too much, in any form, will divert from the process of teaching. Too little will leave the teacher floundering, unaware of the direction she and her pupils are taking.

The Assessment of Performance Unit (APU)[2]

The history of the APU since its first announcement (strangely enough in the Annex to a *White Paper on Educational Disadvantage* in 1974) is a complex, and to some a sinister, story. It is dealt with very fully, and controversially, by Maurice Holt in his *Evaluating the Evaluators.*[3] Brief accounts of its work in literacy and numeracy will be given in chapters 6, 7 and 8. Here, consideration can be given to its activities in relation to the arguments and criticisms given earlier.

Competency and control

Official statements about the Unit have been careful to put the view that it will be taking a neutral 'aerial photograph' of the educational scene, that it will be observing, but not intervening in, the curriculum. That view has, however, not always been maintained either by politicians or professionals.

Thus, the Conservative Party manifesto of 1979, under the banner 'Standards in education', claimed: 'We shall promote higher standards of achievement in basic skills. The Government's Assessment of Performance Unit will set national standards in reading, writing and arithmetic, monitored by tests worked out with teachers and others, and applied locally by educational authorities'.

Similarly, a news issue from the NFER (National Foundation for Educational Research), which has received a large budget for the development of test instruments, says that the APU 'is working to identify standards that pupils might be expected to achieve, and to find acceptable ways of assessing how far they are achieving them' (NFER, 1981). There is thus a fear that the Unit might intervene more than was originally claimed, that backwash, albeit in a positive sense, was part of its function.

This criticism can be answered in a number of ways: teachers and teachers' organisations have been constantly associated with the work of the Unit, and therefore have an opportunity to monitor the monitors; the Government has a right to coordinated information about the state of education in the country; and, if the existing piecemeal assessment situation does not provide such a coordinated picture, it has the right to take steps to obtain one.

Accountability

The Green Paper had, of course, mentioned accountability, particularly to society, and in 1979 a senior member of the Unit included amongst its aims that of providing 'a measure of accountability to the general public given the high level of public expenditure now devoted to education' – a form of economic accountability (Harlen, 1979).

Accountability is also implicit in the model developed by the NFER APU monitoring team, which begins with the needs of society, uses evaluation to check performance against the needs of society, and moves to the significantly named *remediation* which presumably will put things right (NFER, 1979).

Such accountabilities will not arise between individual schools and other agencies, because of the confidential nature of the information. Rather they once more suggest that the Unit could become the vehicle for modification of education generally in the country.

Every pupil

The Unit has rejected – on the grounds of expense, of being unnecessary for a good national picture, and of being positively harmful – the idea of national blanket testing. By means of what is called *light sampling*, in which less than 2% of any age group will be tested in one year in an area of the curriculum, it hopes to build up an ongoing picture of performance. It is estimated that about 5% of schools with 11-year-olds will be involved in each study, and within those schools only one-third of pupils will actually work with the test materials. Thus the dangers of dominating the curriculum are lessened, and the risks of backwash minimised.

Although the light-sampling technique may provide a reasonable national picture and have advantages in minimising disturbing influences on schools, it cannot give information on all pupils. Indeed,

because papers do not carry pupils' names, it cannot provide *any* information to schools about individual pupils. This confidentiality about
schools and pupils is good in avoiding the league tables of over- and
under-achieving schools which have characterised the American
scene, but it does mean that schools cannot turn to APU surveys for
individualised information.

Every subject

So far as the APU is concerned, this has two aspects. Firstly, pupils
who form part of the surveys do not take all of the items in the testing
programme. This reduces the load on teachers and pupil time, and
again produces less interference with the normal work of the school.
Yet, it is claimed, the nature of the items is such that even where
different pupils have taken different parts of the material, the results
can be combined into a meaningful picture.

   More generally, the Unit has met the same problems as were raised
earlier in connection with non-basic areas. The first models for assessment were based on *lines of development* such as the verbal,
mathematical, scientific, ethical, aesthetic and physical – a cross-
curicular model. Work on what later came to be known as *personal
and social development* has, however, now been abandoned, and the
current programme is now *subject*-orientated.

How often?

The APU primary programme at present only involves the 11-year-old
group and, when coupled with the light-sampling technique, can
hardly be held, therefore, to involve heavy testing. It is claimed that,
with the present programme, if 12,000 pupils were required for each
monitoring exercise any one pupil would have only a one-in-four
chance of being tested during his school life.

Notes

1 Lawton, D., *The Politics of the School Curriculum*, Routledge and Kegan
   Paul, 1980.
2 Much APU material is available, free, from: Rm 2/11, Department of Education and Science, Elizabeth House, York Road, London, SE1 7PH.
3 Holt, M., *Evaluating the Evaluators*, Hodder and Stoughton, 1981.

Bibliography

Blackstone, T. and Wood, R., 'Making schools more accountable', *New Society*, 24/12/1981.

Boyson, R., National Council for Educational Standards Conference, Churchill Press, 1973.

Department of Education and Science, 'Education in Schools: A Consultative Document' (The Green Paper), HMSO, 1977.

Harlen, W., 'Accountability that is of value to schools', *Forum*, 1979, Vol. 2, No. 4, pp.287–97.

Holt, J., *The Underachieving School*, Pitman, 1970.

Lawton, D., *An Introduction to Teaching and Learning*, Hodder and Stoughton, 1981.

Marjoram, T., 'The APU', *Education*, 12/1/1979.

National Foundation for Educational Research, 'Monitoring Maths and Language', *Educational Research News*, 1979, No. 29.

National Foundation for Educational Research, 'The APU: A Progress Report', *Educational Research News*, 1981, No. 35.

Stibbs, A., *Assessing Children's Language*, Ward Lock Educational, 1979.

For further thought

1. Do you have standards in education? How would you describe them? Would you try to measure them? If so, how?
2. To whom do you, as a teacher, regard yourself as accountable, and in what way?
3. What steps do you personally take to contribute to a soundly based means of assessment?

For group discussion

1. Too much testing means too little teaching.
2. A national system of education cannot be effective unless it is nationally evaluated.
3. Any teacher with the skill to know her pupils' abilities does not need test materials.

2

The School's Contribution

The previous chapter suggested that any overall assessment system is likely to have many layers. There may be some centrally generated procedures – say by the APU, whose main immediate purpose is reporting at the national level. There may be local authority surveys, either on an every-pupil or monitoring basis, reviewing situations at the area level. More immediately, the school will have its own programme, whether systematic or not, for obtaining feedback on the performance and progress of individual pupils and on the effectiveness of the school as a whole.

Two consequences arise from this layering approach. Firstly, although there is likely to be teacher representation on many of the bodies concerned with testing above the school level, any individual school is likely to be asked to use material which it has had no part in selecting. Secondly, particularly when monitoring only is used, the school may find there are many pupils for whom local or national procedures provide no feedback whatsoever. This chapter is concerned with the general planning of purpose-built school programmes which can complement such beyond-school testing.

Starting points

The school embarking on a systematic programme, or reviewing an existing one, can use its curriculum guidelines to answer questions such as:

– Are there areas which are not currently assessed, either by internal or external means?
– Where there are existing means, are they adequate?
– Where there are no existing means, should there be?

The answers to these questions will be personal to the school, according to its educational philosophy. Whatever they are, they will alert heads and teachers to the possibilities of any major gaps in the network.

Aims and objectives

A major message of this book is that the starting point for a testing programme is not the tests themselves. There must be a previous stage which indicates what the school hopes to achieve for its pupils. Without this, there cannot be harmony between what is taught and how it is tested, and the most expensive and time-consuming programme will only give limited or even distorting information because of the discordance between intentions and evaluation.

How far intentions can or should be specified in advance *and* in detail is a source of much contemporary controversy. A helpful distinction can perhaps be made between *aims* and *objectives*. Aims can be thought of as describing long-term, more general intentions, whilst objectives focus on more immediate ones. Thus we might describe an aim of English teaching as enabling the pupil to appreciate and enjoy reading literature.

An objection to this would be that, though praiseworthy, it is not specific enough either to guide immediate curriculum planning, or any subsequent assessment. Thus, shorter term, more immediate, statements could be made such as: 'to show appreciation of the good and bad points of stories by writing short critiques of books read'.

We have now reached the level of an objective, rather than an aim, and if we make what has been called a 'proximate' goal, related to the immediate and on-going work, we can be even more specific by, for instance, regarding the ability to 'write a critical summary of *Stig of the Dump* in not more than 400 words' as a measure of the pupil's progress, not only in *Stig*-reading but also towards the more long-term, or ultimate goal.

The argument that it is necessary to specify objectives in advance, in some detail, and in terms of pupil behaviour rather than teacher intention, crystallised in America as the *behavioural objectives* movement. At first sight it is a powerful one. Its origins can be seen in the work of Tyler[1], who asked four very pertinent questions:

1 What educational purposes should the school seek to attain?
2 What educational experiences can be provided that are likely to achieve these purposes?
3 How can these educational experiences be effectively organised?

4 How can we determine whether these purposes are being attained?

More succinctly we can divide our planning into:

- *Aims and objectives:* Where do we want to go?
- *Content and organisation:* How shall we get there?
- *Evaluation and assessment:* How shall we know if we've arrived?

Such an analysis clearly suggests that teaching is a directed and didactic activity, aimed at the achievement of certain predetermined targets. Education, on this view, is aimed at changing the behaviour of pupils in specifically prescribed ways.

We have already seen some general arguments against this view: that the processes of education are as important as its products; that there may be unexpected yet valuable outcomes; that educational products are much less tangible than industrial products such as cars and washing machines; that some of them simply cannot be assessed and that the very act of assessment changes what is being assessed.

On the positive side, it can be argued that clear and detailed objectives have the following benefits:

- They enable the teacher, and, if stated publicly, the pupils, to know what is expected to be achieved. They set targets.
- They can thus act as advance organisers which set the educational scene and prevent irrelevant activity.
- Since expected educational outcomes have been clearly prescribed, so too can methods of assessment.
- In sum, they offer clarity: of initial formulation of plans, of ongoing feedback and modification of those plans, and of the means used to assess whether the plans have been achieved.

On the negative side, such objectives can have the following drawbacks:

- By being over-specific, they may trivialise the process of education.
- Since what is tested tends to become what is taught, a programme concentrating on what can be clearly specified and measured may devalue the less tangible aspects of the curriculum.
- Premature and over-planned specification of objectives may blind the teacher to worthwhile but unexpected developments.
- Breaking an activity down into its constituent parts may destroy the very integrity of that activity. Does the writing of endless critiques of specified books necessarily add up to a love of literature?
- The behavioural-objectives approach is tied to a stimulus-response psychology which views the child as a passive agent, *responding*

to the educational programme, rather than actively *participating* in it.

Teachers' views of the 'objectives' model will vary with their view of education. If education is seen as a means to an end, rather than as an end in itself, then it is likely that the logicality of the model will find favour, resulting in an apparently integrated pattern of predetermined objectives measured by predetermined means.

If, on the other hand, education is seen as an open activity, with broad general aims, which may find expression equally well in a variety of content and activity, then assessment procedures are likely to be left more open. This has benefits and dangers. Where a completely *laissez-faire* attitude is adopted, perhaps on the grounds of the criticisms given above, a school may fail to gain profitable feedback – a failure which will not benefit the ongoing educational process. If, however, the 'open' school does value feedback, then the means of obtaining it can arise from the changing nature of the educational activity rather than dominate it from the outset.

A possible parallel might be with approaches to reading. In a scheme such as the SRA Laboratories there is a clearly defined matrix of content, activity and built-in assessment, which largely determines the route followed by the child. The language-experience approach starts, however, from the child, his interests and experiences, and thus there is initially no *precise* specification of content or methods of assessment. But although assessment procedures may not have been precisely defined at the outset, they may still emerge and be used as the language experience programme develops.

Thus, if we believe that the road of education is more important than its destination, objectives will be less clearly prescribed to allow for profitable byways, and hence assessment procedures will be less clearly specified initially. But it will still be possible for the teacher to assess what is being achieved, both during and at the end of the process. The essential difference is that the criteria will emerge as the activity unfolds.

At the start of a project, for instance, a teacher does not know exactly how each child will react, in what specific direction he will go. But she does have a backcloth of expectations of what she hopes will be achieved, and can assess progress against this, and against any new developments which arise. In effect, the project is its own assessment, although, as we shall see, systematic criteria can be applied to it.

What to test: the use of taxonomies

The impressive word *taxonomy* simply means an orderly classification, often hierarchical in nature – that is, moving from lower to higher orders. In looking at the aims and objectives of education, it is often helpful to break larger areas into smaller units. We are then mapping the educational territory so that we do not miss our way. There are many published taxonomies, both for education as a whole, and for particular areas such as reading.

The best known is Bloom's *Taxonomy of Educational Objectives*[2], which runs to several pages, and covers the cognitive, affective and psychomotor domains. It is thus a major and comprehensive classification, but from it some general threads can be extracted to show how even a simple classification can act as a guide both to teaching and testing.

Bloom divides his cognitive domain into six main areas – knowledge, comprehension, application, analysis, synthesis and evaluation. Four of these will be considered here, and reference back to them will be made when particular subject areas are considered.

Knowledge

Knowledge involves the acquisition of specific facts, or of general principles: we can recite the twelve times table, we can rehearse Archimedes' Principle.

Comprehension

Comprehension in Bloom's terminology, implies that we can understand the material presented, without necessarily being able to relate it to other material. Thus, we might advance beyond the level of mere repetition of Archimedes' Principle to being able to relate it to objects floating in water, this being the situation by means of which we learned the Principle. But we might be entirely baffled when asked to extend it to a hot-air balloon.

It is important to distinguish between knowledge and comprehension. Most students are aware that they can get by in exams by regurgitating carefully remembered material which they by no means fully understand. Similarly, in project work it is important to check that a pupil's carefully gathered facts do have some meaning for him. In chapters on reading and number we shall move on to distinguishing different levels of understanding or comprehension.

Application

Application occurs when we *can* transfer and generalise principles freely from one situation to another. Thus, the child who can confidently cope with addition on the planet 'Oneandland' (which, of course, has a five-base system) *without* having been specifically taught to do so, demonstrates his ability to apply, or generalise, his knowledge of place value outside the particular system (e.g. the ten-based system) in which he first met it. Application is thus a situation-free form of understanding, in contrast to the situation-bound comprehension as used by Bloom.

Evaluation

Evaluation implies the existence of the other levels, and is thus the highest process in the taxonomy. It involves checking for internal consistency (e.g. that a passage does not contradict itself), for credibility, and against other sources of information. Some writers suggest that this level is scarcely reached by most primary children, but it is the author's belief that this view underestimates young children's ability to think critically – which is the essence of evaluation.

Even so short a classification may help us to go beyond the level of knowledge – though knowledge, being insidiously easy to test, does tend to dominate. Programmes such as *Top of the Form* and the more elevated *University Challenge* do not, in essence, go beyond this level (though intelligent anticipation may help with our 'starters for twenty'). Even the *Mastermind* series show little more than an infinite capacity for rote memory.

A case study

Classifications can be much more detailed than the brief outline given above. As a case study, we can turn to some aspects of the Schools' Council project on place, time and society.[3] 'Integrated' work means notoriously different things to different people, and often rightly so in view of the environment and resources available. The project thus suggests a framework within which teachers can place their own situation.

It begins with two major divisions: skills and personal qualities. Skills include the intellectual, social and physical strands. Since we have briefly looked at the cognitive domain of Bloom's taxonomy, we can compare it with the project's intellectual strand. This, in turn, is divided into six subdivisions:

1. The ability to find information from a variety of sources in a variety of ways.
2. The ability to communicate findings through an appropriate medium.
3. The ability to interpret pictures, charts, graphs, maps, etc.
4. The ability to evaluate information.

5. The ability to organise information through concepts and generalisations.
6. The ability to formulate and test hypotheses and generalisations.

We can quickly see that aspects of Bloom's framework are implicit
here. The pupil is to obtain information (i.e. knowledge); he is to
interpret (i.e. comprehend); he is to evaluate, and he is to generalise
(i.e. apply). But these are at present *aims* rather than objectives: they
do not tell us, for instance, just what a pupil would be doing to con-
vince us that he had the ability to 'find information'. Thus, if we are
going to be more precise, we must proceed further. Here is one
teacher's breakdown of this general objective:

Finding information

What to look for:
- Uses contents page and index.
- Looks for more than one source.
- Looks for different kinds of source (maps, interviews, pictures, etc).
- Checks one source against another.
- Can find sources available inside school.

Now we have turned the aims into general objectives and thence
into more specific ones. We could, if we wished, refine these even
further – say to make reference to *specific* sources within the school –
but many teachers would feel things had gone quite far enough already, thank you.

Notice that the classification has not prescribed any *content:* it is
concerned with the process, in this case intellectual, that the child will
show and achieve using the content as a vehicle. If the content, as is
so common, were the major theme of a classification there would be
a real risk that the sole process (if it can be called that) would be
knowledge. On the other hand, there must be some content – children cannot find information unless there is something there to start
with, they cannot evaluate without material. Thus we can move to a
'content-process' model which lists the expected content against the
processes to which it might give rise (see Fig. 2.1).

Such a model can be used when planning work, when observing
work, and when recording the results of the work. A typical example
is that of a teacher involved in the project. He decided that he would
check his beautiful workcards (the content) against some of the objectives (the processes) that the project suggested. He found that the
overwhelming majority of the 20 cards simply asked the child to find
specific information, and communicate it through writing, or

Content ⟍ Process	Living Things	Measuring Scales	Daily Life	Materials
Evaluation				
Application				
Comprehension				
Knowledge of Generalities				
Knowledge of Specifics				

Figure 2.1   A content-process model, from *Assessment in Education*, D.G. Lewis, Hodder and Stoughton, 1974.

occasionally by a picture. He hastened to extend the set to cover somewhat higher objectives!

Such a classification can also guide the assessment of ongoing work. Instead of looking at the topic folder simply as a product, the teacher can examine the processes which went into it (*Did* the child manage to combine different kinds of information effectively?) and record their detail as she sees fit. This will in turn enable her to plan further work to extend and balance objectives, and, at the end of the year, can be used as a summative record both for individuals and the class as a whole (though it is, of course, important that the next teacher understands the classification!)

In setting up a classification:

– don't passively crib one from a book – firstly it might not suit *your* purposes, and secondly, it must have meaning to *you* in terms of your children and their work;
– equally, don't try to pluck one out of the air; look at examples and *then* move towards your own;
– in checking on the aims and objectives, list them as activities pupils will *do*; and
– don't make them so detailed that you have to ask the Head for an ancillary to help in recording.

Finally, even if you recoil from detailed classifications, at least don't reject them entirely: education *is* something more than the acquisition of knowledge.

Why test?

The purpose, or the 'why?', of testing is implied in the definition given earlier. Quite simply, testing exists to provide feedback. But the school must also consider to what use the feedback will be put. A more detailed analysis of feedback will now be given.

Reporting

One immediate result of feedback is, of course, that it can lead to *reporting*, – to stating how things are. In turn, this may go outside the school – to a national agency, to the local authority, to parents – or it may remain within the school for the benefit of the teacher, her colleagues, and the pupils.

Furthermore, reporting could refer only to the immediate state of affairs (*contemporary reporting*) or it might refer to a developing process (*consecutive reporting*). For an individual pupil we might want to know what his reading level is at a particular time (contemporary) but it would also be useful to know how it is developing (consecutive). The one is a snapshot, the other a film.

Guidance

Put this way, reporting may sound rather passive, simply commenting on what has happened so far. But teaching is an organic and not a static affair. Teachers are *not* simply commentators: they are themselves part of the action. Hence reporting within the school should serve as *guidance*.

Base-line tests will help to start the pupil off at an appropriate level and on an appropriate course. Ongoing formative tests will check whether that course is being maintained, or whether changes are needed to bring the pupil (or possibly the teacher) back on course. Sometimes, it may be necessary to change course in view of the feedback about progress.

Finally, end-of-course or summative testing, besides summarising past performance, may also serve as a pointer for the future. The teacher as tester is thus a Janus figure, looking at the past to see what has been done, and towards the future to see what should be done.

A particular feature of this forward-looking task is that of *prediction*. We do not suppose that tests are simply a random sample of pupil behaviour, but rather that they are indicators of an ongoing process of development. Thus what we learn at present may help us to anticipate what may happen in the future, and hence guide future teaching.

There are, of course, objections to these expectations, notably by Rosenthal and Jacobson in *Pygmalion in the Classroom*[4]; for example, that they may harden into self-fulfilling prophecies bringing about the very changes they predict. Whilst there are many criticisms of their work, there is a danger that teachers allow the results of testing, or indeed first impressions, to blind them to changes ('Oh, he's a slow learner, if ever I saw one. He'll not change'). Here lies the value of an open mind, accepting the results of a test as a guide, but using further, ongoing testing to check on the original 'forecast'.

It has already been pointed out that teaching is an active, and not a caretaking, process. Thus, when reporting and predicting give gloomy forecasts, we do not have to accept these fatalistically. We hope to do something to refute them to remedy things. Hence reporting, the stage of *description*, can lead to that of *prescription*. When the forecast is set fair, we prescribe the mixture as before. When it is poor, we change the medicine.

Diagnosis and attainment

Besides looking at testing, in relation to time, as an immediate or an extended process, we can also consider it in relation to depth. How much do we want to know about a pupil? Is an assurance that his reading is average for his age sufficient? Or do we want to know in more detail about his reading?

In the testing of *attainment* we are looking at the overall picture, summarising the situation, whereas in *diagnostic* testing we are looking for specific areas of strength and weakness, searching for the obstacles preventing the child's smooth progress. It does not of course follow that we use diagnostic testing only when attainment testing alerts us to below average performance. A child may have an average or above average level in reading, as judged by the crude yardstick of an attainment test, yet have deficiencies whose removal would lead to even greater progress.

Attainment summarises *performance,* diagnosis indicates *patterns* within that performance: if attainment is the naked eye of testing, diagnosis is the microscope.

Comparison: normative and criterion referencing

Another reason for testing might be that of *comparison*. But, like the gentleman who was asked how his wife was, we must answer 'Compared with what?' Technically, the two major methods of comparison are known as *normative* and *criterion*. Norm-referencing, as it is often called, facilitates comparison between pupils, whereas criterion-referencing compares the pupil's own *individual* performance with some definite level or standard.

Criterion-referencing

The driving test is often cited as an example of a criterion test: provided a certain standard is reached, as measured by success on a given set of checks, you pass. It does not matter in the least how you stand in relation to other drivers: the comparison is only with the standard set.

Many 'proficiency' awards for life-saving, judo, for ballroom dancing, athletics and gymnastics rest on the testing of performance against a given standard. The elementary award of the Squash Rackets Association prescribes performances such as: 'To serve correctly four services out of six attempts from each service box where the ball hits the opposite side wall behind the short line and bounces in the correct back quarter of the court'. Here we have very clearly specified criteria – a behavioural objective really – and provided the player satisfies the criteria, he gets his award. It does not matter whether he is a county junior champion, or a beginner, or whether he lost his last six matches in a row: the competition is with the standard, not with other players.

The teacher may, however, wish to complement this referencing of her pupils' achievements against a list of criteria by instead referencing them – and implicitly, therefore, her own teaching – against the achievements of other pupils. A simple method of doing this is by *ordering* the pupils, either by the allocation of marks or grades, or on the basis of general impression. But this has at least two major flaws.

Firstly, within the classroom, we cannot assume that the 'distance' between, say, pupil 1 and pupil 2 is the same as that between pupil 10 and pupil 11 on the ranking: nor can we assume that the difference between a teacher's marks of seven and nine is the same as that between her marks of five and seven. Because they are not tied to any definite scale, these marks and rankings lack anchorage – they are not clearly referenced except in terms of the individual teacher's own judgements.

This then leads to the second problem: that of comparison between the judgements of different teachers. Even if a teacher were able to construct a satisfactory scale within her own classroom, her scale would be very unlikely to be identical with that used by other teachers teaching children of the same age elsewhere.

To use a physical analogy, it would be like measuring pupil heights in terms of the lengths of the teachers' arms. Only if we can find a scale which goes beyond the subjectivity of individual measurement techniques can we adequately compare pupil performance in different classes and different schools.

Norm-referencing

Norm-referencing offers a solution to this dilemma by establishing a large reference group whose level of performance is known. The performance of individual children, or groups of children, can then be referenced against these established standards, thereby complementing the judgement of the classroom teacher by offering a wider and more objective comparison.

This comparison normally takes two forms. Scores typical of, or average for, children of different ages may be quoted, so that we can match the performance of a pupil against a set of age-related scores (as in 'reading ages').

More recently, most tests have quoted 'standard scores', explained more fully on p 56. These are so arranged that any given score – say 125 – represents the same standing (in relation to the appropriate reference group) wherever the pupil is, however old he is, and whatever the subject being tested. Here, then, we have a very portable teacher's arm which can not only move from class to class and school to school, but also reach from subject to subject.

In recent years, there has been a swing from normative to criterion comparison. The arguments supporting this swing are varied.

- Normative comparison invites (though it does not necessarily involve) competition, whereas in primary schools at least, education is seen as an individual rather than competitive venture.
- Normative tests frequently, though not invariably, give only a global score which gives little help in pinpointing an individual pupil's strengths and weaknesses.
- Thus they may be said to focus on individuals as members of groups, rather than in their own right.
- Normative tests are often tied to a psychometric model of human ability which implies a certain definite distribution of ability – the so-called 'normal curve'.
- This may lead to a philosophy of failure – 'We must give some E's to get the curve right'.
- Criterion testing focusses on the individual, and hence can more easily give clear pointers to individually designed educational programmes.
- It can avoid overtones of competition between pupils and their consequent implications of failures. When allied to 'mastery learning' it concentrates on helping the pupil to do what he cannot at present do, rather than allocating him as a success or failure in relation to what other pupils do.
- It is not necessarily tied to any preconceived notion of the distribution of human abilities.

The arguments are however by no means one-sided. It is not so much a question of *either/or* as one of choosing the right comparison for the right purpose. To answer the question, 'Is John doing as well in

reading as in number?', strict criterion-referencing would not be helpful. We might say, 'Well, he knows his number bonds to 20, and in
phonic development he's happy with initial consonant blends'. But
how do we compare those two criteria?

Normative comparisons, when derived from standardised tests, enable performance in different subjects, by different pupils, to be compared. Further exploration of the uses of the two forms will be given
in later chapters, and the deeper mysteries of the 'normal curve' will
also be revealed.

How to test?

Formal or informal?

One major distinction in the 'how' of testing is betwen *formal* and
informal methods. The formal technique may be described as the set-
piece of testing, when a definite decision has been made to test, often
using material prepared in advance either outside or within the school.
In contrast, the informal occasion may arise during the work of the
class, and may be spontaneous in nature, as when a teacher asks a child
to explain the workings of a model he has made.

Again, as with the other divisions, there is not a black and white
division; rather there is a continuum, from the pomp and circumstance
of the 11-plus, through the weekly spelling test to the quiet exploration
of a child's problems with division.

It does not follow, either, that all external tests are formal in nature,
and all home-grown ones informal. Many externally produced tests,
such as the Nuffield Foundation checkups in mathematics, suggest
procedures which necessitate the minimum of interference with normal classroom activities – indeed they may arise directly out of them –
whilst at the other end, a school may sometimes have end-of-term
tests, produced internally, but distinctly formal in their administration.

Objective or subjective?

A second division is that between *objectivity* and *subjectivity*. Here,
though, there is again no hard and fast boundary: it can be said that
objective tests reduce the differences between situations and testers,
whilst subjective procedures are less concerned with overall comparability but more with the possibilities of individual judgement. Thus,
where all children have the same explanations for a test, the same time
to do it, and the answers are marked in such a way that no ambiguity

can arise – then, whoever does the marking, we have a form of objective test. When a teacher hears a child read, with no external yardsticks to guide her judgement, we have a much more subjective assessment.

Subjective appraisal carries the possibility of a sensitive interaction between assessor and assessed – say when a sympathetic hearing is given to a slow learner's (objectively) frail little story. It carries with it the dangers of variability of standards, of idiosyncratic interpretations, and of a possibly too personal approach.

Objective testing avoids many of these dangers, sometimes at the cost of a more impersonal interaction. It does not follow though, that a subjective assessment is sloppy and an objective one harsh. We shall see that assessment by the individual teacher can be rigorous and systematic, yet sensitive to the individual situations of pupils.

Internal or external?

Apart from those areas where some form of secondary selection still operates, primary schools are singularly unfettered by the chains of external examinations. There is, however, a large body of published tests upon which the schools can, if they wish, draw. Indeed, the title of this book may have led readers to think only of external, published tests. This is far from its intention.

As stated in the Preface, the notion of testing implied is that testing has occurred whenever a teacher obtains effective feedback on a child's progress, performance or personality. Sometimes this feedback will come from the administration of a published test. Sometimes it will come from a few seconds exploration of a child's work. Both have their place in an integrated system; the expertise and time invested in the construction of published tests does not necessarily mean they are the only adequate form of testing, and in the next three chapters the advantages and disadvantages of internal and external sources will be considered.

Notes

1   Tyler, R., *Basic Principles of Curriculum and Instruction,* University of Chicago Press, 1949.
    The Behavioural Objectives model is examined in Lawton, D., *An Introduction to Teaching and Learning,* Hodder and Stoughton, 1981, Ch.7.
    A fuller treatment is given in Davies, I.K., *Objectives in Curriculum Design,* McGraw-Hill, 1976, and Rae, G. and McPhillimy, W.N., *Learning in the Primary School,* Hodder and Stoughton, 1976.
2   Bloom, B.S., *Taxonomy of Educational Objectives,* Longman, 1956.
    Its application to test construction, together with the 'content-process'

model is given in Lewis, D.G., *Assessment in Education,* Hodder and Stoughton, 1974, and Morris, L. and Fitzgibbon, C.T., *How to Measure Achievement,* Sage, 1978.

3   Cooper, K., *Evaluation, Assessment and Record Keeping in History, Geography and Social Science,* Collins, 1976. Other short frameworks which may help the teacher to construct objectives outside the basic areas are: Inner London Education Authority Guidelines: *History in the Primmary School, Social Studies in the Primary School, The Study of Places in the Primary School.* (ILEA publications are available from: ILEA Publishing Centre, Station Road, Highbury, London N1).

4   Rosenthal, R.R. and Jacobson, L., *Pygmalion in the Classroom,* Holt, Rinehart and Winston, 1968.
For a more general treatment, see Pidgeon, D.A., *Expectation and Pupil Performance,* NFER, 1970.

For further thought

1.   Do you feel that the journey of education is more important than its destination? In other words, are you for or against defining objectives at the outset of a unit of work? Or do you have different feelings according to the curriculum area?
2.   'The House of Intellect is not just a pile of bricks.' How could a programme of objectives avoid this criticism?
3.   Think about some of the situations in which you have assessed children recently, either formally or informally. What was the purpose of the assessment? Do you think others in the same situation would have reached the same conclusion? If not, what would cause the variation?

For group discussion

1.   *Role play*: A representative from a firm publishing tests arrives, with an impressive folder of material. Explain to him your reservations about over-use of external tests. He, in turn, explains their advantages.
2.   Ask a (young) member of your discussion group to do a forward roll. Examine how you could apply *normative* comparison to this, and how you could set up a *criterion-referencing* situation.
3.   Ask a member of the discussion group to sing a short song. Assess the performance (a) on a scale of 0-100, (b) by general impression, with printable comments.

3

External Sources of Assessment: Published Tests

As the title implies, we are concerned in this chapter with material originating from outside the school. In the main, this is of two kinds: examinations set by bodies other than the school itself, and published tests distributed by a company or testing institution. Since the impact of external examinations on the primary school is small, we shall be concentrating on published test material.[1]

An initial classification

There are a variety of ways in which such external material may be classified. Several possible headings have been briefly explored in the previous chapter. The following may help to systematise more detailed consideration:

- Content: the skills, knowledge and understanding being tested.
- Function: what the test does.
- Comparison: either with the performance of other children, or with given standards or skills in a particular area.
- Individual or group.
- Availability: open to all educationalists, or restricted to more specialised users.

Content

Immediately after the Second World War, the predominant pattern of testing in the primary school, reflecting the selection procedures then in use, focussed on 'intelligence', English (including reading) and mathematics. With the decline of selection, and changed views on the nature of 'intelligence', the last two have become dominant. Science, geography and history are scarcely represented in primary catalogues, though material is available for the secondary school.

On the less strictly academic side, there are instruments, such as the *Junior Eysenck Personality Questionnaire,* but few if any primary schools make use of published tests in this area. Thus the basic skills are most likely to be assessed by means of published tests, leaving physical and social studies, as well as general behavioural assessment to be covered, if at all, without the aid of external material.

There are, however, some sources of assistance for the school which desires a more all-round survey. Thus, Lindsay's *Infant Rating Scale* (1981) can provide information in five areas: language, early learning and motor skills, behaviour, social integration, and general development.

It will be seen that this greatly widens the range of assessment beyond the purely scholastic. It is also a benefit that all the parts of the package come from the same stable – in other words, the *Infant Rating Scale* is a coherently designed instrument. It might be possible, therefore, to obtain the same range of content by using a variety of tests from different sources, but this, as will be seen later, could have serious disadvantages.

Inevitably, the use of a wide-ranging package is likely to cost more, in time and money, than the administration of one or two short tests in the basic skills. There is thus a balance to be held between what is invested and what is gained, and this brings us back to the general questions of Chapter 2: what facets of pupil development do we want to assess, and how much time and effort do we want to put into the enterprise?

Function

The difference between the resumé provided by an attainment test and the greater detail of a diagnostic one has already been outlined. Published tests of both types are frequent, with the accent mainly on attainment. Ideally, of course, the two functions work together so that, where the tests are designed to work in harness, there is, as with the *Infant Rating Scale* described above, a greater coherence and compatibility betwen the elements.

In the number field, for instance, the *Basic Number Diagnostic Test* (Gillham, 1980) is deliberately intended to complement the 'attainment' function of the *Basic Number Screening Test* (Gillham and Hesse, 1976). We thus have a planned programme of interaction between the two tests. Sometimes this planning will extend very widely indeed: the Daniels and Diack *Standard Reading Tests* (1958) is an example of the 'battery' approach.

The *battery* in this case consists of an attainment test of oral reading, followed by 11 other tests. Depending on the level of the child's performance in the attainment test, one or more of the later tests will be given to check more fully on a particular aspect of reading. Cross-references can also be made between the diagnostic tests themselves, and they can be used to check more fully on difficulties the teacher may have noticed in the child's class reading. A battery thus offers a network of interlocking tests focussing on different but related aspects of pupil performance.

Related to the diagnostic function is the *profile* approach. In this, a range of sub-tests is provided, aimed at assessing different aspects of performance in a given area. Thus the *Edinburgh Reading Tests* will give an overall score, summarising the child's general level in reading, but they can also provide sub-scores on the separate tests, enabling comparison to be made of performance *within* the individual as well

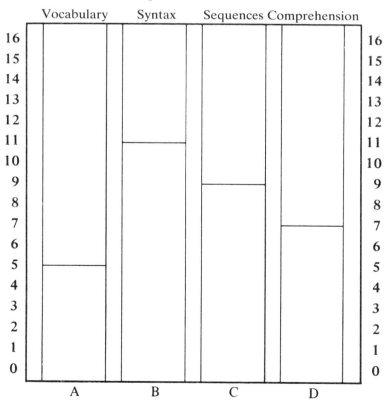

Figure 3.1 A sample profile comparing performance on different sub-tests of the *Edinburgh Reading Test*, Stage 1, Hodder and Stoughton, 1977.

as *between* individuals.

If so desired, a profile can actually be drawn, highlighting visually the pattern of performance, as in the example in Figure 3.1 from *Edinburgh Reading Test, Stage 1*. Whilst caution must be used in interpreting the differences between sub-tests, there is the opportunity to explore more fully test performance, though again with a greater outlay than required by a shorter, single test.

If the word 'diagnostic' does not figure in the title of a test, it may still serve that function. Sometimes, as with Carver's *Word Recognition Test,* the attainment function can be supplemented by the teacher's scrutiny of the child's responses, leading to a greater knowledge of his particular weaknesses. In this test, Carver has deliberately included the diagnostic function by a careful choice of material. In other cases, no diagnostic function may be claimed but the test, used sensibly, can yield diagnostic clues. Thus, a careful record of a child's errors on the well-known *Schonell Graded Word Reading Test* can add something to the knowledge of a child's reading age, although, of course, the diagnostic function is not a fully-designed one.

Comparison

The great majority of published tests still offer normative comparison. Most often, this is by comparison of an individual score with that of a large group of children of the pupil's own age – nine-year-olds being compared with nine-year-olds, and so on. Sometimes, however, the comparison, as with a reading age, will be with the performance of a typical child of a given chronological age. A child scoring 21 on the *Southgate Group Reading Test 1* obtains a reading age of seven years, zero months. This means that his score is equal to the average score of the seven-year-olds who were used for the original standardisation of the test. The child himself might be six or eight, so that the comparison this time is not necessarily with pupils of his own age.

More recently, tests have tended to combine the normative and criterion comparisons. This is not an entirely new development, since the Daniels and Diack Tests already mentioned can perform both functions. In their book, normative data is given by the provision of a conversion table for converting marks into reading ages, but the criterion function can, perhaps more importantly, also be utilised. Daniels and Diack argue that reading develops qualitatively – in a series of levels – and that the score gained by a child can be used as a criterion to judge whether a child has or has not reached a particular level. Seven 'standards' are given for these levels, and these, as described by the authors, summarise what has been achieved, and give pointers to what is needed for the move to the next standard.

The two authors write:

> Children in Reading Standard III are at a critical stage of learning the skills involved in reading. They have already achieved a fairly high degree of understanding of the fundamentals of reading; they have grasped the fact that there are a number of exceptions to the rules— 'special' words. They have now to add to their repertoire the full list of more complex phonic 'rules', beginning with such diagraphs as *th, oo* and *or*. There are also the rules about the distant modification of vowels, e.g. *cap* becoming *cape*, the sound of the *a* being modified by the distant *e*, whilst the *e* itself is not pronounced. The test most useful here is Test 7E, the test which ranges over all these phonic rules. Tests 8 and 9 should also be given at this stage.

(From *Reading Standard III* (RA 6.1–6.5 years)

A similar, though less detailed, approach has been used by Spooncer in *Group Literacy Assesment* (1981). Here, a raw score may give normative information – both standard scores and reading age equivalents can be obtained – or it may be used as a criterion for the allocation of the child to one of four categories of competence in literacy skills. These categories can then be used both to indicate the child's likely performance, and give pointers to appropriate provision in the future. Once more, it is important to learn what functions the test is supposed to perform, and how far these match the intentions of the user.

Availability

Whilst many tests can be freely used by teachers and other educationalists, some will only be released to individuals having prescribed qualifications or experience.[2] The former class is normally known as 'open', the latter as 'restricted'. The restricted class may be further subdivided in terms of the rating of the user. The NFER has three main categories:

1. Available to all qualified teachers.
2. Available to teachers with further training in test use (sub-divided into five levels of availability according to experience and training).
3. Specially restricted and research tests.

A 'Qualifications of test users' form must be completed to establish an individual's position in these categories. Teachers should, therefore, check what restrictions may apply to tests in which they are interested.

The construction of a published test

Quite apart from considering the particular type of test which might be purchased, it is, of course, entirely relevant to ask what one is buying when purchasing a published test.[3] Behind the test papers and manuals which arrive at the school there will be a considerable investment of time and expertise which could not be expended by practising teachers. The steps towards the final version of a test are long, and it may well take two or three years to bring an idea to fruition. Some of the major phases are described below.

Selection of test content and function

It is clear from the discussion in Chapter 1 that no responsible test constructor would design a test just for the sake of it: a new test must adequately fill a need in the schools. Ideally, there should be a close liaison between teachers and testers, the former making clear their needs, and the latter supplying the time and expertise. The development of the present author's *Group Literacy Assessment,* for instance, was largely due to the clearly expressed feelings of secondary teachers about the difficulty of collating the different types of information provided by their feeder primary schools, and their desire for a short but effective means of assessing the literacy skills of their intake.

This sounds clear-cut, straightforward, and no doubt very praiseworthy. In practice, however, the test constructor is in a far more difficult position than the teacher in the school. The teacher knows what has been taught, how it has been taught, what has come before, and what will come next. The constructor is dealing with a 'distant' audience, with a range of schools having a range of differences in content and method, and cannot hope to tune in to all these variations as those on the spot might be able to do.

As a simple example, if one school highlights understanding in the teaching of mathematics, whilst another concentrates on computation, it is difficult for the constructor to satisfy both in a single instrument. Thus Pidgeon (1972) says: 'The range of objectives covering mathematics learning at the end of primary school is so wide that it would be impossible to ask any individual pupil to take a test which aimed to measure them all'.

Let us suppose, however, that it is clear a new test would be a useful addition to the teachers' resources, and that the general range of application has been agreed. The next step is to think about the content in more detail.

Construction and selection of a preliminary set of items

The format of items for particular purposes will be discussed in later chapters. The general point here is that no-one expects to hit just the right mixture of items first time. A large pool of items will be produced, taking into account the age and ability of the pupils, the content areas to be sampled, and the type of function desired (e.g., providing information on pupils of a wide range of ability or on a narrower band, such as those in need of remedial help).

The number of items is likely to be from two to three times that of the final version. A few may be discarded when discussion shows them to be hopelessly ambiguous, but the test constructor will largely operate on the practical argument that the proof of the pudding is in the eating – that is, he will try them out on groups similar to the intended or target groups. This is usually called the pilot stage, and in fact there may be several pilot runs (for the author's *Group Reading Assessment,* no less than nine!), with content and format being refined constantly in the light of feedback from these initial trials.

Selection of items for final version

In selecting the items which will form the final and published version, several criteria will be applied, some to the series of items as a whole, and some to individual items. Firstly, there will be the need for the test scores to show a good spread. There would be little point in constructing a test of 50 items if most children scored between 20 and 25. There should be an opportunity for the less able children to score, but equally there should be an opportunity for the brighter children to show just what they can do.

If a test bunches children at the bottom, many scoring zero or very low scores, it exhibits the 'floor' effect, and reveals very little about them. If it bunches children together at the top, with many scoring maximum or very high marks, then it shows the 'ceiling' effect, and again fails to give as full information as it might. The cartoons here may indicate why these terms are used!

Ideally, if the test is to cover all ranges of ability, the constructor will be aiming at a smooth curve of distribution, with the average children clustered near the middle range of marks, and smaller and smaller proportions scoring towards the extremes (see Figures 3.2 and 3.3).

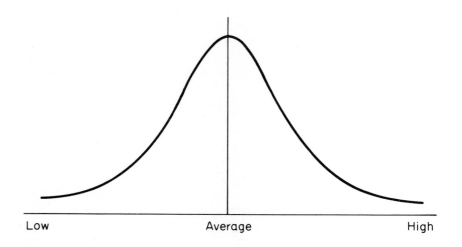

Low   Average   High

Figure 3.2 A smooth, symmetrical curve

Tests which are heavily 'skewed' (having high proportions of very high or very low scorers) will need adjustment for the reasons given above. To make the adjustments, the constructor will turn to individual items, and scrutinise very carefully how each behaves, as described below.

Item analysis

In conventional test design, a sample of papers which represents in miniature the range of scores in a pilot study will be studied for two important figures – one concerned with the ease or difficulty of each item, and the other with the extent to which the item differentiates between high and low scorers on the test as a whole. The first is known as the 'facility index', and the second as the 'discrimination index.'

The facility index
Though tedious, the facility index is quite easy to calculate. The successor or failure of each child on each item is recorded, and this index is simply the percentage of children getting it right. Thus, if we have taken a sample of 200 papers, and the first item is answered correctly

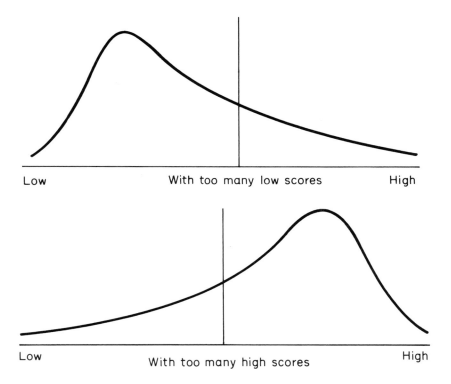

Figure 3.3 Skewed curves

on 120 of them, its facility index is 60%. If item 20 is answered correctly by only 70 children, it has a facility index of 35%.

You may like to look at Figures 3.2 and 3.3 again and consider how the skewed distributions could be made more symmetrical by the appropriate exclusion or addition of items. In passing, spare a thought for the constructor: if she has a test of 60 items and analyses 200 papers, she will have scrutinised 12,000 items!

The discrimination index

This requires a rather more complex calculation. The papers are arranged in order of *total* score and the proportion of those with high scores who pass any given item is compared with the proportion of low scorers succeeding on the same item. Often, the total sample is divided into three groups on the basis of total score, and the percentage of passes from the high group (the upper third) is compared with that in the low group (the lower third). The method, therefore, is often known as that of 'upper and lower thirds'.

To calculate the index, we subtract the passes in the lower third from those in the upper third, and divide by the number of papers in each third. Thus, if each third contains 50 papers and 40 children pass item 19 from the top group, whereas only 20 pass it from the lower third, the item has a discrimination index of (40–20)/50, or 0.4. If all of the top group pass, whilst all of the bottom fail, the index has its maximum value of + 1.0. In the freak case where all of the lower third pass, but all the upper fail, we would have an index of −1.

Clearly, it would be reasonable to expect that if all the items are pulling together in measuring the same ability, discrimination indices would be positive, and preferably quite high. The constructor, therefore, would reject any items showing a low, or negative, value. Teachers who have doubts about some published items should remember that they have all been subjected to intense practical testing and analysis: the constructor does not put them in just because he subjectively feels they are 'good' ones.

This is only a very rough sketch of the procedures used to ensure that the final items chosen are the most suitable for their purpose. There will be problems, especially in timed tests, with items which are not attempted by some children, with guessing in multiple-choice tests, and with the extent to which the distractors in a multiple-choice version are actually considered by the children. At last, however, the long initial labour is over, and a final set of items has been chosen.

Standardisation

Since the data derived from administration of the final version will serve as a reference point for several years, it is important that the standardisation procedure is carefully designed.

Firstly, the reference group should be large. It is no use getting 40 or 50 children of the right age and using these. Modern tests frequently use standardisation groups of 3,000 or more.

Secondly, the group must be well chosen. A group, however large, which does not reflect the type of child on which the test will actually be used will give misleading results. For instance, it would obviously be foolish to standardise a test designed for use in State schools within the private sector only.

There are a number of ways of attempting to secure an adequate reference or standardisation group. In the first, an attempt is made to reflect the characteristics of the target population in the standardisation sample. Thus, where it is hoped that a test will have a national usage, there will be a determined effort to ensure that the composition of the standardisation sample reflects national characteristics – e.g., in the balance of schools from large and small conurbations, in the proportion of boys and girls. The following quotation from the Manual of the *Edinburgh Reading Tests* may illustrate the care taken:

In England and Wales, two representative authorities (one a county authority, and the other a metropolitan district authority) were chosen from each of ten areas. A random sample of five schools was chosen from each authority. A single class was then selected from each school, to give an average class enrolment of 30 within each authority. The classes were also selected to give an equal balance between the sexes, and to give as even a distribution as possible across the age range 7:0 to 9:0. In the very few cases where classes were streamed, care was taken to obtain a balanced representation.

Clearly, so detailed and lengthy a procedure is outside the scope of a school, and may well be worth the price of the materials. A second procedure, which involves less expenditure of time and effort, might be called the 'saturation' method. In this, all the pupils within a particular area (say a county borough) who are of the desired age are tested. We thus obtain information on almost 100% of children from a *limited* region, as compared with the fraction of children from a range of regions by the previous method.

The second method was used in designing a series of tests for Kent, for use within that county, and by the present author in constructing his *Group Reading Assessment* and *Group Literacy Assessment*, both of which were standardised in county boroughs.

The advantages and disadvantages of local and national standardisation are discussed in the section on Interpretation (pp 56–7). Whichever method is chosen, there will be a large reference group whose scores are available for the final stage of preparation of conversion tables, etc.

The normal curve
We come now to what is, for the general reader, a somewhat technical section. However, since the principles of the normal curve underpin many other aspects of testing, it is well worth while spending some time on it.

If we took a large group – say a thousand – of men of a given age, we would find that the distribution of their heights followed a smooth symmetrical curve, highest in the middle, and smoothly decreasing away from the centre or average. The shape of the curve can be defined by a (fairly complicated) mathematical formula which essentially predicts the frequency at any given distance from the average, or mean. From this, we can then determine what proportion of the men in our group were equal to, or smaller than, a given height.

From the illustrative graph at Figure 3.4, we can see that 2% of the men were 5'4" or less, 16% were 5'6" or less, 50% were 5'8" or less, and so on. We summarise this by saying that, for the distribution, 5'4" is the second percentile – meaning that we have included 2% of our

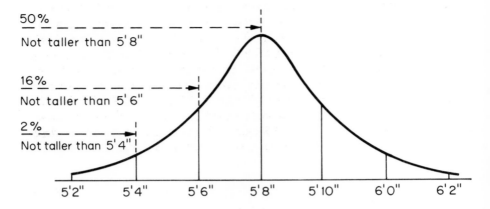

Figure 3.4

groups as we move from the shortest height to 5′4″. Now *if* (and it may be a big 'if') we can express other human characteristics in the form of this mathematical curve, we can determine an individual's standing in the group (i.e. use normative comparison) by his distance from the mean.

It is extremely unlikely that the constructor's test scores, even from his final administration, will conveniently follow the curve, so he has therefore to calibrate them so that they do. To do this, he takes a number of percentiles as markers – that is, he finds the raw score at and below which a given percentage of his standardisation group has scored. *Moray House Tests* take 15 such points, from the second to the hundredth, which can then be equated with standard scores. The correspondence between raw scores, percentiles and standard scores for an imaginary test is given in Table 3.1.

Table 3.1 Scores on the 'Darts' Test of motor coordination

Raw Score	% of children scoring at or below that score	Standardised score
19	2	70
35	16	85
48	50	100
60	84	115
75	98	130

Table 3.1 indicates that 2% of children in the standardisation group scored 19 or below – that is, 19 was the second percentile, whereas 16% scored 35 or less, and so on. So far, so good: but why does a raw

score of 19 become a standard score of 70? The answer is because modern test constructors have agreed that for comparability of scores, it is desirable to settle on a definite mean and a definite spread of scores. Most published tests have a mean of 100 and a 'standard deviation' (i.e., a measure of spread) of 15. This means that – whatever the subject being tested, whatever the nature of raw scores – 2% of the standardisation group will have fallen at or below a *standard* score of 70, 16% at or below a standard score of 85 etc. Table 3.2 gives the percentage of children in the *standardisation* group scoring at or below given standard scores. This will be true whatever the original raw score distribution, the type of material, or age of the children.

Table 3.2

2% of children fall at or below a standard score of	70
10%	80
25%	90
50%	100
75%	110
90%	120
98%	130

It can be seen that 50% of children fall between standard scores of 90 and 110 (an interval of 20) whereas only 23% fall between standard scores of 70 and 90. This indicates, as we have already seen, that scores are bunched more closely about the mean of 100.

In practice, this 'normalising' process will be carried out on the raw marks of children of almost exactly the same age – children aged nine years three months will be compared with all other children of that age in the standardisation group and so on at monthly intervals. The final result is a smoothed conversion table with which teachers are no doubt familiar (see Table 3.3).

Standard scores confer considerable advantages in comparing and combining marks in a way which is not possible with, say, the marks of an internally produced test. How this directly helps the teacher is explained in Chapter 4.

Reliability and validity

Two further pieces of evidence are needed before the information for the manual is complete. These concern the terms *reliability* and *validity*.

Reliability

A variety of terms – dependability, stability, consistency – are used to indicate different facets of this concept. Basically, they reduce to

Raw Score	Age												
	10:6	10:7	10:8	10:9	10:10	10:11	11:0	11:1	11:2	11:3	11:4	11:5	11:6
60	96	96	96	96	95	95	95	94	94	94	93	93	93
61	97	97	96	96	96	95	95	95	95	94	94	94	93
62	98	97	97	97	96	96	96	95	95	95	95	94	94
63	98	98	97	97	97	97	96	96	96	95	95	95	94
64	99	98	98	98	97	97	97	96	96	96	96	95	95
65	99	99	99	98	98	98	97	97	97	96	96	96	95
66	100	99	99	99	98	98	98	97	97	97	97	96	96
67	100	100	100	99	99	99	98	98	98	97	97	97	96
68	101	100	100	100	99	99	99	99	98	98	98	97	97
69	101	101	101	100	100	100	99	99	99	98	98	98	98
70	102	102	101	101	101	100	100	100	99	99	99	98	98
71	102	102	102	101	101	101	100	100	100	99	99	99	99
72	103	103	102	102	102	101	101	101	100	100	100	99	99

Table 3.3 Conversion table from raw scores to standardised scores, *Group Literacy Assessment*, F. Spooncer, Hodder and Stoughton, 1981. A pupil aged 10:6 with a raw score of 60 obtains a standardised score of 96. To obtain the same standardised score at 11.6, a pupil needs to score 67.

two major points. Firstly, we would hope that the results of a test administered twice to the same children within a short interval of time would not show major inconsistencies in their relative positions, or in their scores. We would not consider a test very reliable if it placed Mary first one week and last the next, or if Johnnie's reading age dropped from ten years to seven years over a month.

This stability aspect can be measured by administration of the same test twice, though this is open to criticism because of the 'practice' effect of children having worked the test before. More stringently, a 'parallel form' (a test of similar design standardised on a similar group) can be used, and the scores or ranks of the children can be compared on the two versions.

The self-consistency of a test measures the extent to which the different items pull together in the direction of the test as a whole. A team of horses in which one insisted on pulling in a different direction to the rest would scarcely make a reliable driving force! To assess this, the child's single test paper can artifically become two parallel forms, by, for instance, comparing his total on the odd-numbered items with those on even numbers. This is the so-called 'split-half' technique (since we have split each single test paper into two halves).

The constructor can alternatively use a formula known as 'Kuder-Richardson 20' to calculate the similarities in scores of all possible halves of the test, rather than the single-half described above.

The result of any of these measures will be expressed as a correlation which can vary from +1 (complete agreement between two sets of scores) through zero (only chance agreement) to −1 (complete disagreement – the top score in one testing is the bottom of the other, etc.)

Modern test constructors will be hoping for a reliability coefficient of at least .90 for an educational test to be used in schools, and frequently report figures as high as .95 or above. The importance of a high reliability coefficient for the interpretation of individual test scores is explained in the next chapter.

Validity

The test constructor, and indeed the test user, will probably be expecting the test to measure something definite – say, computation in number or phonic skills in reading. To some extent this can be estimated by looking at the content of the test – at the kind of items it contains. This is the *content* validity. Sometimes, as with a new form of reading test – say, a cloze procedure – users may need convincing that the test is a valid (i.e., a true) measure of what it claims to measure. To provide this reassuring evidence, a comparison will again be made, but this time with *other* sources.

A typical example can be provided from the standardisation of the author's *Group Literacy Assessment.* The raw scores of 2,544 children, who took both the new test and the established Daniels and Diack *Graded Test of Reading Experience,* were correlated to give a coefficient of 0.80. Again, as with the reliability coefficient, the higher the figure the greater the degree of agreement – in this case between the two independent measures of the same children. Because the figure found is reasonably high, we can accept that it is likely that something in common is being measured by the two tests. This form of validity is known as *concurrent* because two measures are taken at the same time.

Predictive validity is less often quoted, since this measures the extent to which a present performance agrees with some later one – and a new test will often of course have been published too soon after its completion for this information to have been gathered. For an educational test, the constructor will be looking for a validity coefficient of 0.80 or above.

The essential difference between reliability and validity can be summarised by saying that in reliability we compare the test with itself, whereas with validity we compare the test with some outside measure of the same skill.

Notes

1   The tests referred to in this section are:
Carver, C., *Word Recognition Test,* Hodder and Stoughton, 1970.

Daniels, J.C . and Diack, H., *Standard Reading Tests*, Chatto and Windus, 1958.

Eysenck, H.J., *Eysenck Personality Questionnaire (Junior)*, Hodder and Stoughton, 1975.

Gillham, W.E.C., *Basic Number Diagnostic Test*, Hodder and Stoughton, 1980.

Gillham, W.E.C. and Hesse, K., *Basic Number Screening Test*, Hodder and Stoughton, 1976.

Godfrey Thomson Unit, *Edinburgh Reading Tests*, Stage 1 (1977), Stage 2 (1972) and Stage 4 (1977), Hodder and Stoughton.

Lindsay, G.A., *Infant Rating Scale*, Hodder and Stoughton, 1981.

Moray House College, *Edinburgh Reading Test*, Stage 3, Hodder and Stoughton, 1973 and 1982.

Schonell, F.J. and F.E., *Schonell Reading Tests*, Oliver and Boyd, 1942 to 1955.

Southgate, V., *Southgate Group Reading Tests*, Hodder and Stoughton, 1959 and 1962.

Spooncer, F., *Group Literacy Assessment*, Hodder and Stoughton, 1981.

Test publishers are usually willing to supply specimen sets of tests for teachers to inspect.

2   Catalogues of tests, and details of their availability, are readily obtainable from publishing houses such as:

Heinemann Educational Books, 22 Bedford Square, London WC1B 3HH.

Hodder and Stoughton Educational, Mill Road, Dunton Green, Sevenoaks, Kent, TN13 2YD.

Macmillan Education, Houndmills Estate, Basingstoke, Hants, RG21 2XS.

NFER-Nelson Publishing Company, Darville House, Oxford Road East, Windsor, Berks, SL4 1DF.

3   Readers wishing to explore more fully the technical aspects of test construction can consult:

Child, D., *Psychology and the Teacher*, Holt, Rinehart and Winston, 1977, Chs. 13 and 14.

Lewis, D.G., *Assessment in Education*, Hodder and Stoughton, 1974, and, for a very thorough treatment, Satterly, D., *Assessment in Schools*, Basil Blackwell, 1981.

Normative referencing is clearly explained in Childs, R., *Norm Referenced Testing and the Standard Score*, NFER, 1977.

Bibliography

Pidgeon, D., *Evaluation of Achievement*, Macmillan Education, 1972.

For further thought

Take one or two tests designed for the age range you teach, and then:
1. Read the test manual in the light of the headings on pp.30–2 to establish the 'intentions' of the test constructor.
2. Look at the test material and consider whether it would adequately serve those intentions in your own situation.
3. Return to the test manual to establish the statistical 'credentials' of the test (see p.37). You may think this is too technical an activity for a practitioner, but it is important for the proper use of tests, and therefore for pupils' educational future, that you do not form wrong notions of how tests work. So persevere, and return to this book (or others referred to here) if you are stuck.

For group discussion

A teacher should test her own teaching. Divide the material from p.34 onwards amongst the group, each person explaining to the group her own section (e.g. item selection, and analysis, standardisation, the normal curve, reliability and validity). Then devise questions which will test the efficiency of the explanations.

4

External Sources of Assessment: Choosing and Using Tests

The previous chapter introduced several of the major concepts of test construction and use, and these will now be related to specific school needs and purposes. Although we are still considering tests imported from outside, it should be remembered that many of the concepts relevant to published tests – notably reliability and validity – are equally important for school-produced assessment, as will be shown in Chapter 5.

Choosing a test

Content questions

What do we want to test? If we have clear idea of our objectives in an area of the curriculum, then we can try to match our chosen test to our objectives.

Firstly, we can check the approach and content of the test against the school's approach and content. Schools will not be giving themselves or their children a fair chance if, for instance, the balance of skills tested by an English test bears little relation to the balance aimed at by the school.

Secondly, the content can be checked for 'ageing' – that is, the presence of outmoded or even inaccurate items. The Daniels and Diack Test 12 (1958), for instance, contains the following: 'In this country, the commonest fuel used for house fires is (wood, oil, smoke, coal).' That is a somewhat difficult one for the child whose home is centrally heated by oil!

Similarly, the *Neale Analysis* (1958) has a story about a milkman's horse which wandered in the fog: again, not a familiar experience to present-day children. These anachronisms do not of course necessarily mean that the test cannot be used effectively. On the other hand, if a more recent test does the task as well, then it may be preferred.

Age of pupils

Who do we want to test? Some tests concentrate on a narrow age band, whilst others cover several years of school life. The author's *Group Reading Assessment* (1964), for instance, is aimed principally at the first year of junior school, whereas Vernon's *Graded Word Spelling Test* (1977) gives norms from 5.6 to 17.6 years, thus encompassing practically the whole of school life.

The advantage of the 'narrow' approach, particularly where a skill may be changing in nature as the child gets older, is that it can focus on the skills most important at a given age, and provide content and style relevant to that age. Its disadvantage is that some other tests will have to be used later in the child's career, with consequent problems of comparison between performance on different tests.

These problems of comparison may be lessened if an adequate wide-range test can be found, since there should be a greater coherence and consistency of results derived from the same test than from an assortment of tests. Such a test, however, would either have to be longer, and therefore more expensive, or, if of the same length as a narrow-range test, would have less items per age group, a factor known to reduce reliability.

Some tests can be used above their main age range for the testing of slower-learning children. This has the advantage of giving them a chance of success on a larger number of items, rather than only one or two on a test designed for their own age range, but it can lead to problems of content: what may be an adequately stimulating item for an average seven-year-old may be insulting, in content if not in difficulty, to a slow eleven-year-old, and thereby diminish motivation and give a deflated impression of his performance.

The 'floor' and 'ceiling' effects are also important in relation to the age of the pupils. If a group is at the lower end of the stated suitability range, and particularly if it is known to be somewhat below average, then the use of the test will lead to a crowding of scores at the lower end, and a consequent loss of useful information, with a number of children perhaps not scoring at all. Conversely, with a bright group at the top end of the suitability range, some children may hit the ceiling, and it will not be possible to tell how much better they might have done with a more extensive testing. Such criticisms have been levelled at the use of *Reading Test NS6* with older pupils in national surveys.

Purposes

Comparison within the school
Sometimes we may want to compare children within a given class or school. If, for instance, there is any kind of allocation to groups (say for reading) then an objective test will aid such grouping. We have already seen that there are objections to the risks of 'labelling' a child prematurely and the teacher should be open to later signs of change in the status of children in relation to others. The test is, after all, a guide and not a god.

Comparison outside the school
At other times, we may wish to compare internal performances with some regional or national standard. A published test is particularly helpful for this purpose, since, as indicated in Chapter 3, great care will have gone into the choice of an adequate reference group. Where, as with many *Moray House* and NFER tests, there has been a national standardisation, we can relate individual or group scores to the national norms as derived from the particular reference group.

Where a test is used throughout an authority, it may be possible to create a local standardisation. This will have the advantage that any individual or group comparison will now be on the basis of information derived from the year group being tested, and not from schools in other areas at other times. A disadvantage is that there will be no indication from local norms of how an area or school compares with national standards.

The benefits of both types of comparison can be obtained by using a test which has national norms, and having it restandardised for the particular year group being tested. The Godfrey Thomson Unit, authors of the *Moray House Tests*, for instance, will provide local norms if information on the raw scores of children is given in a pre-scribed form. With a *Moray House Test* we can have the benefits of a national reference group together with an up-to-the-minute standardisation on 'our own' children.

There are, of course, certain dangers in school-to-school comparison. If 'league tables' of named schools are drawn up, they may be misinterpreted by lay people who may not appreciate that a 'below average' performance from a school with all the odds stacked against it may really be a quite impressive feat.

Most authorities using large-scale testing are, however, careful to keep results anonymous where any published results are used, but can communicate personally to heads how their school stands, what proportion of children are markedly above or below the local average, and so on. In addition, the authority gains a picture, derived from the same test, of performance within the area, which can guide the allocation of resources. Such a picture would be hard to collate using a variety of different tests. An example of an 'anonymous' set of results is given in Table 4.1.

Table 4.1   Simplified example of a reading survey report

School	Mean score	
1	42.3	
2	41.7	
3	40.4	
4	40.2	
5	40.2	
6	39.0	
7	38.0	— Borough average 38.0
8	37.8	
9	37.5	
10	34.0	
11	31.2	— National average 33.0
12	28.4	

Comparison of successive year-groups
Either by comparison with an outside standard, or simply within the school, we can compare one year's intake with another ('Is this year's intake as good as last year's?') or we may ask whether the reading standards of fourth-year leavers are rising or falling. Here an important point must be made: standards cannot be compared in any satisfactory way if different tests are used for the comparison. It does not matter that we have used two tests, both labelled as 'reading tests' and that both are aimed at, say, fourth-year junior groups.

From all the advice given in the previous chapter, you will realise that the tests may sample different content areas, may have been standardised on somewhat different reference groups, and may perhaps differ in the way they spread the scores of pupils.

Comparison: normative or criterion?
The essential question to bear in mind here is: do we want to relate our children's performance to that of a large carefully chosen group, or do we want to compare them with measures of competence in a given area, independent of their standing in relation to other children? If the first, then we will be looking for a test giving standard scores, attainment ages and a good spread of pupil scores. If the second, we require a instrument which presents a ladder of achievement, so that we can plot how far an individual pupil has climbed. Once more, we cannot expect the test to help us if its function does not fit our purpose.

Comparison: over time

Here we are really talking about progress, and trying to answer questions such as 'How much progress has Johnny made in reading this year?' or 'Has this year's group benefitted more from the new methods than last years's did with the old approach?' We may be wanting objective support for statements on record cards and reports summarising what has been achieved over a school year.

As with other comparisons, we must beware of the simple-minded assumption that, because we have given the same child or the same group two (different) tests, we can directly infer progress from the change in scores over time. The problems of compatibility of content, of approach and of reference groups will still obscure an objective comparison.

We have already seen that the use of parallel forms of a test can avoid many of these problems. One form can be used early in a year and another later. Another useful approach is to use tests which derive from the same source, and have been standardised on similar reference groups. Thus Young's 'Y' Mathematics (1979) tests form a series deliberately designed to be used in successive year groups, and with the advantage of having been developed in the same schools. With such a coherent approach, we can more firmly rely on 'consecutive' information than when we use a variety of tests from different sources, developed in different areas.

Two further technical effects are relevant to the successive testing of progress. The first is the *practice* effect. We know that a second try commonly produces a better performance, without any additional training. If children take the same test at too frequent intervals (say more than once a term) then their improved scores may simply reflect over-familiarity with the material, rather than true progress, and we shall be misled as to the real gains being made. Parallel tests will obviously help to reduce this effect.

The second, slightly surprising, effect of successive testing is that of *regression to the mean*. With normative tests which have the same mean and spread, there will be a tendency for those who make high standard scores on the first test to be placed lower on the second. Conversely, those who make low scores on the first testing will tend to rise on the second, as indicated in Figure 4.1.

Not all individuals will follow this trend but, on average the movement will be towards the mean or average score. Thus, a child who has done really badly on a test at the beginning of a year may appear to have improved simply because of the inevitable statistical consequences of normative comparison.

Screening and surveying

Both for the local authority and the school, screening and surveying can be useful. The first refers to the selection of pupils whose per-

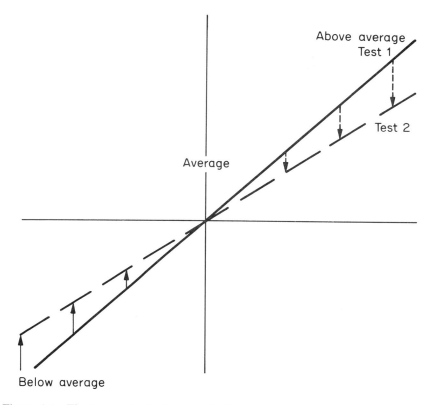

Figure 4.1   The 'regression to the mean' effect.

formance differs sufficiently from the average to suggest that some form of special provision might be helpful, and normally is applied to children who are not progressing well – for example, in the selection of poor readers for remedial help. As a process, however, it can also be applied to the selection of gifted children for some form of enriched programme.

With a *screening* procedure, the question of a smooth, symmetrical distribution may not be paramount, since what we are really doing is a kind of sieving, like that used to grade apples. We may want small apples (i.e. low scorers) to fall into our net, and are not so concerned with the size of the remainder of the produce. Thus, it may be possible to use a test for younger children, provided its content is sufficiently motivating. As compared with a test having a more 'normal' distri-bution, lower-ability pupils will score over a wider range of marks, thus enabling us to discriminate more finely between them. Against this, however, is the likelihood that there will be a severe ceiling effect for abler children, so that if we used such a test on a year group, we might get little valuable information on many of the pupils.

No educational screening procedure can be perfect because no set of test procedures is completely reliable. Even the elaborate methods of the 11-plus produced misses as well as hits. Children allocated to grammar schools failed to make it, and others sent to secondary modern schools showed by their progress that they might well have been better placed in the grammar school. 'Misses' will, therefore, be of two categories: those we place in a 'competent' category, but whose later progress shows they are not so, and those who are placed in an 'incompetent' category, but who later prove to be above that level. Our 'hits', of course, will be those we correctly place (see Figure 4.2.).

	Prove to be 'competent'	Prove to be 'incompetent'
Placed in 'competent' category	HIT	MISS
Placed in 'incompetent' category	MISS	HIT

Figure 4.2   The hits and misses of screening.

A single test should *never* be relied on for the allocation of a child to a particular category, since different tests will undoubtedly produce different groups of children as 'competent' or 'incompetent'. An application of the screening procedure to the selection of remedial readers is given in the case study in Chapter 6, page 90.

A *survey* approach, unlike screening, tries to provide information right across the range of ability. Here, therefore, we shall want a test which provides headroom and a good spread of scores. Thus, the author's *Group Reading Assessment* designed for first-year juniors will survey efficiently at that level, and can indeed be used to screen for poorer readers at the end of primary education. But it would be a very poor test to use for surveying fourth-year juniors, since a large percentage of them would make full, or nearly full, marks on it. The school would, therefore, be expending time and money on getting inadequate information for their purposes. Figure 4.3 shows what may happen when a test is used for surveying outside its proper age range.

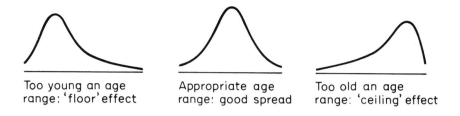

Figure 4.3   Surveying outside the proper age range.

It is, of course, possible to combine screening and surveying if a test is available which gives an opportunity for *every* child to perform at his appropriate level, and which also gives sufficient discrimination amongst the group to be screened to minimise the risk of misclassifications.

Group Reading Assessment (1964), and *Group Literacy Assessment* (1981) (designed for fourth-year juniors and first-year secondary pupils) will both survey and screen *if used with the proper age range.*

Economic questions

How much money and time do we want to spend? There is little point in going to the expense of buying a published test if the same evidence and assistance can be obtained from material generated within the school. In other words, we must look at what the user of the test will get in return for the expense of buying it. This expenditure can be considered both in terms of money and time.

Money

Here we can ask what the cost will be of *all* the material needed for administration of the test (i.e. the manual, the test papers, marking template, etc.). The *NFER Reading Test DE* cost, in 1983, £9.85 for a class of 30 children. The school may then ask whether the information obtained is worth the price or whether some other form of reading assessment might be cheaper, releasing money for the purchase of a test in another field.

This form of argument may underlie the continued use of the individual *Schonell Graded Word Reading Test,* since once a copy is purchased, no further outlay is needed – but this may be a very false economy, as will be shown in a moment. It is, however, worth finding out whether the test material is reusable (for instance, booklets which have separate answer sheets can be used again) or not, as in the case of test forms on which the children write their answers.

Time

How much time do we want to spend? This involves expenditure, but in a less obvious way. An example would be in the testing of a class's reading. Clearly, to test each child individually will consume much more time than using a group test. Whilst a group test could be completed in 30 minutes or so, several hours might be taken up by the individual test. During that time, the teacher is not available to teach her class, or if some other person does the testing, then they are being withdrawn from circulation.

Some teachers may feel it worthwhile to get individual contact with their pupils, and might be willing to spend time getting to know a child's reading by personal encounter rather than by the less personal evidence of a written group test. Attitudes, persistence and confidence are difficult to assess by a group test, but may appear in an individual one – though some children may well prefer the anonymity of the group situation to that of individual exposure.

If we do decide on a group test, then besides the administration time, that of *marking* must also be considered. A longer test may take longer to mark but may also give much fuller information. Modern test manuals often give average marking times, and estimates can also be obtained from the sources mentioned in the notes.[1]

With some tests, marking time can be decreased or even eliminated. Many now offer a *template* which can be placed over the child's answer sheet, so that the right answers made by the child can be seen at a glance. (For multiple-choice tests, such a 'screen' can be made by the teacher by cutting windows in a plain sheet at the appropriate points, though double underlinings may have later to be checked.)

A newer development – again only applicable to multiple-choice tests – is that of machine scoring. The child uses a special pencil and the paper is fed through a machine which automatically gives his score. More recent developments of this technique offer a package of statistical calculations – such as averages for classes or schools, performance on particular items, etc. – which, if the information is required, greatly reduces the time spent by teachers. Although the form of the test is necessarily restricted, an authority using a large number of tests for a survey might find this approach both economical and rapid.

Quality
How good is the test? To get to know a test, the best technique is undoubtedly to purchase a specimen set, which will normally include a test paper and a manual. A careful look at these may well save much frustration.

The first aspects the teacher will want to inspect are probably those of a practical nature – administration and marking. Nothing is more irritating than to find ambiguous instructions, or an involved marking key which has to be consulted so often that smooth marking is impossible. We must thus consider:

- the clarity of instructions, both for pupils and teachers;
- the ease of marking; and
- the procedure for scoring 'productive' responses (i.e., those where children enter their own answer rather than select one from those provided).

Having established that the test content and administration are suitable for our purpose, the statistical information can be reviewed. This is normally towards the end of the manual (presumably because many teachers don't use it!) but it is well worth seeking answers to the following basic questions:

Was the standardisation group large and well-chosen? (Be cautious if the evidence is not available or only vaguely given.)

Was the standardisation recent?

Are the figures for reliability and validity (see p.41 if you've forgotten) respectably high?

Have comparisons been made with other tests which you or your colleagues have found to be valuable?

Using the test

Administration

If the advice of the previous sections has been followed, there should be little difficulty in administering the test fairly and accurately. What should *not* be done is to walk into the room with an unopened manual and a handful of test booklets, and improvise from then on. We should know beforehand the maximum number of children that can be tested at one time (which might mean splitting classes), whether any particular equipment (pens, pencils, rubbers, rulers) is or is not allowed, what information needs to be completed before the test starts, whether a watch with seconds hand is required, etc. Professor Vernon's advice in the directions for his *Graded Word Spelling Test* can scarcely be bettered:

> Please read through the directions carefully at least twice before attempting to test. Underline the main points that need to be remembered, and follow them as accurately as possible.

During the test, a watchful eye should be kept for copying and for the child who turns over two pages or waits at the end of a page when he should have continued. With a test of several sections, there is the need to prevent the child who finishes quickly from going back over previous items if this is not permitted. There is also the need for the child who finishes early to be usefully occupied without distracting the others.

When the test has been completed, the same care must be given to the marking. Where clear-cut answers are provided, no special cases should be allowed, however plausible they may seem to the teacher. Ideally, the test should be re-marked by a second marker or at least a spot check of a sample of papers should be carried out.

These may seem pedantic suggestions but, in the author's experience of reviewing thousands of scripts marked by teachers and by himself, a surprising number of marking errors, failures to transfer sub-totals properly, failures to follow the marking key and even failures to conform to specified time limits have occurred. There is little value in paying for an objective test only to ruin its objectivity by careless administration.

Interpretation

Let us, however, pat ourselves on the back for our careful and zealous administration and marking. What are we now going to do with all those scores? To some extent this will depend on what the manual offers. For a norm-referenced test, this is likely to take one or more of three basic forms:

1. The standardised score

As we have seen, modern tests arrange the scores of their reference group so that they follow a very definite mathematical curve. This will usually have a mean of 100. It does not, however, follow that if a child scores more than 100 we can necessarily describe him as 'above average', or if a school averages 95 that we can consider it 'below average'. It all depends which average we are talking about – which reference group we are using. All we can legitimately say in the absence of other information is that the score we are considering is above or below that of the average for the original reference group, i.e., 100.

An actual example may reveal some of the problems of interpreting scores, and suggest a possible solution. Let us suppose that a borough uses a test with national norms (as printed in the manual) for selection purposes, but decides to have the benefit of a recent and local standardisation as well. Teachers will then be confronted with two conversion tables, one relating to national, the other to local, standards.

If the area is an educationally affluent one, there may well be a gap of up to ten points betwen the score a child achieves using the national conversion, and the lower one derived from local norms. Similarly, the average standard scores for the authority may well be several points above 100. Subsequent users of the scores must be very careful how they interpret these sets of scores.

The score of a poorer child might give him a standardised score of 84 on national norms but only 75 on the local ones. Secondary heads receiving a figure in the 70s might well be thinking that they are receiving a child of borderline ESN level yet, in terms of nationwide comparison, the child is in the dull-to-low average band.

There need be no problem if the nature of the comparison group is borne in mind. If it is not, the objectivity of standard scores may be lost in a quicksand of confusing interpretations. The use of 'yardsticks' (as on p.49) may well provide the anchorage points needed.

2. Percentiles

These may be quoted separately from the standardised scores or can be derived from them, as in the table on p.41. They describe 'how far up' a pupil's performance is in relation to the reference group – the 40th percentile means that 40% of the *original* group reached or fell below that level of performance. Again, we must be careful to remember what the reference group is. To take the previous example, a pupil might well be placed at the fifth percentile in comparison to the local standards but as high as the 20th in relation to national standards.

3. Attainment ages

Here, the point of comparison is the performance of a typical or average child of a given chronologic age. Some test producers, such as the NFER, do not offer this information, but the author, in company with some other test constructors, believes that there is a meaning in, say, a reading age which cannot so easily be derived from the more abstract standardised score. The teacher has a 'feel' for what a child with a reading age of eight years is likely to be capable of, and in effect the age serves as a kind of criterion – has he or has he not reached the level of an average eight-year-old?

But again, we come across the tricky problem of 'average'. Who, what or when is this 'average' child? The series of national surveys conducted from 1948 to 1972 suggested that standards of reading were changing, which in turn suggests that the 'average' child of the 1980s will score at a different level from his counterpart of the 1950s.

Some tests, such as Schonell's, were originally standardised over 40 years ago and the original norms can, therefore, hardly be described as contemporary. Now if the standards of reading have *risen,* an average child today will score more than his peer of 40 years ago, but if the original norms are used he will appear to be above average! The complexities of the problem can be seen from the various restandardisations of the Schonell's *Graded Word Reading Test* which have been made in recent years.[2]

Notes

1   A 'consumer's guide' to reading tests is published, for instance, by West Sussex County Education Committee, *Assessment of Reading Difficulties,* or Northamptonshire Reading and Language Development Centre, *Reading: Which Test?*

A comparison of group reading tests is made by Nichols, R., 'A comparison of four group reading tests in surveying the attainment of first and second year junior children', Centre for the Teaching of Reading, University of Reading.

2   The table below shows how a given raw score (i.e. the number of words read correctly) will earn a different reading age on *Test R1* according to which standardisation table is used:

Words read correctly:	5	25	45	65
Reading age:				
'Original' Schonell	5.6	7.6	9.6	11.6
1978 Schonell	6.5	7.7	9.2	10.8

Those wishing to cover more fully the various restandardisations of the *Schonell Test R1* can consult: Shearer, E. and Apps, R., 'A restandardisation of the Burt-Vernon and Schonell Graded Word Reading Tests', *Educational Research,* Vol. 18, No. 1. In commenting on the relative difficulty of the words, Shearer and Apps note that 'canary' moved from 36th to 45th in difficulty, while 'statistics' eased from 85th to 74th.

Test Bibliography

Daniels, J.C. and Diack, H., *Standard Reading Tests,* Chatto and Windus, 1958.
Neale, M.D., *Neale Analysis of Reading Ability,* Macmillan, 1958.
Spooncer, F., *Group Reading Assessment,* Hodder and Stoughton, 1964.
Spooncer, F., *Group Literacy Assessment,* Hodder and Stoughton, 1981.
Vernon, P.E., *Graded Word Spelling Test,* Hodder and Stoughton, 1977.
Young, D., *Y Mathematics Series,* Hodder and Stoughton, 1979.

For further thought

1.   Consider recent occasions when you have used the term 'average'. Was its meaning always clear to you, and to your audience?
2.   Construct a questionnaire type form to evaluate published tests, using the framework of this chapter or one of your own making. (Although concerned with teaching rather than testing materials, the following may be found helpful as an example of a detailed assessment schedule: Peters, M.L. and Cripps, C., *Appraisal of Current Spelling Materials,* Centre for the Teaching of Reading, University of Reading.)

For group discussion

Teachers concerned with the same age range should present details of the tests they use (e.g. for reading and number), giving their reasons and the advantages of the material. Ideas can thus be exchanged.

5

Internal Sources of Assessment

Although published tests offer the school the benefits of time and expertise beyond its own resources, they cannot by themselves form a comprehensive assessment programme. Teachers can complement their external sources by providing a different form of expertise, based on their own on-the-spot and intimate knowledge of curriculum and pupils. Care needs to be taken with internal assessment, however, if the advantages of external objectivity are not to be clouded by over-subjectivity within the school.

The value of internal assessment

The principal advantage of using internally generated procedures has already been indicated: they are devised by those who originally planned the curriculum and, therefore, objectives and the means adopted to achieve those objectives are known. The interests and abilities of pupils are also known so that there is a greater possibility of 'tuning-in' by internal assessment in a way not so easy with an imported test.

But if the advantages of internal sources – avoidance of the 'backwash' effect, more intimate relation of curriculum to assessment – are so great, why bother to use external sources at all? One strong counter-argument to this 'hands-off' policy highlights the problem of subjectivity and the acceptance of the teacher as the sole arbiter of assessment. It can be argued that the assessments of an individual teacher, or a single school, are taken from a very special standpoint and might not agree with those made by others in the same situations. This can certainly be presented as advantageous, since the assessor is appreciating something of which he is part rather than something external and even alien to him.

It does, however, mean that whenever comparisons need to be made betwen classes or between schools, there is a risk of confusion of standards. Any head who has read reports compiled by a variety of teachers will appreciate the range of expectations and judgements exhibited even within a small primary school. However certain we may be of the value of internal assessment, we may have to accede to the use of external material on *some* occasions.

There is, of course, a dilemma here: the over-use of external tests may inhibit the freedom of the classroom teacher by imposing an external set of objectives, whilst over-reliance on internal measures may introduce unreliability in the form of inconsistency between the standards of different teachers. The remainder of this chapter will be devoted to a consideration of forms of internal assessment, with suggestions for improving their consistency.

Forms of internal assessment

Observation

Observation is surely one of the most powerful techniques in the teacher's repertoire. All the working day she is observing children, either intentionally or incidentally. It has the advantage of allowing behaviour to occur naturally, rather than in a highly structured situation such as a formal test, and can be applied not only to academic skills but to attitudes, interests and the general development of personality. It forms the basis of comments on record cards, reports, and of the school's general impression of its pupils. It is part of the working knowledge used by all teachers, but does need to be consistent in its purpose. An examination of factors leading to inconsistency may lead us to ways of being more consistent. Amongst the major factors are the following: *time, structure, expectation, the 'halo' effect, and a lack of an appropriate reference group.* Ways of overcoming the problems presented by these are summarised at the end of the section (p.62).

Time
Faced with the problem of rating children's behaviour, a research team might devise a careful time-sampling schedule by which each child was observed, using the same criteria, for the same length of time in similar types of situations to all others. Teachers cannot be so impartial in their observations. Some children need more attention than others (often for disruptive reasons) and thus the sample of teacher observations may, willy-nilly, prove to be biased. Again, independent

observation teams have observation as their main task, unlike the teacher who shares it with teaching, organisation and the maintenance of a good classroom climate.

As a simple example, if a teacher were to observe each child in a class of 30 for only three minutes per day, it would use up about one third of her teaching time. We thus have two problems here: the general one of availability of time, and the more particular one of scanning the whole class without artificially distorting the natural flow of teacher attention ('Oh dear, I haven't looked at Molly for 4 hours 13 minutes.').

Structure
A particular problem facing the teacher in the primary classroom is the change in structure which has occurred over the last 20 years, and particularly since the Plowden Report. She meets very varied and flexible situations, a rapidly changing scene, during her day's work so that her observations are likely to be of an *ad hoc* rather than a pre-planned nature.

Where open-plan or integrated-day methods are used, there may be different children engaged on different tasks at different times and at different places – all of which make systematic observation difficult. The teacher's own natural interests may contribute to this, in that she may spend more time interacting with children working in her own preferred subject area rather than in one in which she has less interest. Thus she may have a wealth of observations from number work, but a less complete set from English activities.

The inevitable incompleteness of teacher observation, even within a fairly structured situation, was shown by a classroom survey which found that, during reading periods, only ⅔ of the children's activity was directed towards the 'official' reading material, ⅓ being devoted to 'diversionary activities'.[1]

Expectation
The expectations a teacher brings to her encounters with children may affect the outcome of those encounters, both in assessment and actual performance. In a study of reading, for instance, children were given an objective test, and teachers – in ignorance of the results – rated the children for reading. It was found that middle-class children were rated as superior in reading to working-class children, even when both had the same objective score. Similarly, studies in the infant school have suggested that teachers group children in terms of perceived social class.[2]

Halo effect
In some ways, the 'halo' effect is a form of expectation: good performance in one area tends to produce 'good' assessments in others. The

'glow' from one area spreads to other aspects, causing the pupil to be rated more highly in them than may be objectively merited. At the other end of the scale, it is possible to 'give a dog a bad name' so that, for instance, isolated acts of poor behaviour may cause a lower estimation of academic work than is warranted.

Lack of appropriate reference group

We saw in Chapter 3 that published tests often use a large, carefully selected, reference group as a backdrop against which the performance of any individual pupil can be seen. The classroom teacher cannot refer to so large or so representative a group. Her immediate reference group will be her class of 30 or so with whom she spends most of her working week. At the back of her mind will be memories of many more children encountered during her teaching exerience. This personal contact may make her an excellent reporter on her own class (particularly if she heeds the notes above!) but problems may arise when a comparison between classes is needed.

The remedial teacher might well write 'excellent work' in commenting on a pupil, and be sincere in that comment against the backdrop of her own class. But that same work, placed against the mainstream backcloth, would probably be below average. Other teachers, new to a particular age group, might not have had time fully to set their sights, and may thus have different yardsticks from the 'old hands' of the year. When a comparison between children from different classes in the school is needed, and particularly if that information is going outside the school, say to parents or to secondary schools, it is important to try to iron out these variations as much as possible.

Assisting teachers' assessments

Teachers are not research workers, and it is not suggested that they should play at research by developing an elaborate scheme of observation. However, many will be only too aware of the yawning gap which occurs when some children's blank report forms appear before their weary eyes. 'What on earth can I say about him?' is a sign that the balance of observation has somewhere gone wrong, that someone has slipped through the net. Hence ways which ensure that each child has reasonable consideration will assist both the ongoing work of the class and the preparation of summative reports. The teacher could, for instance, adopt a 'rolling diary' in which notes on three or four different children are written each week in rotation. This does not mean that Sir or Miss's heavy breathing is upon their necks each moment, but that they are particularly kept in mind during that week.

A number of ways can be used to encourage teachers to cover roughly the same ground in their observations. Whilst guides, checklists and inventories should not become strait-jackets – since neither teachers nor pupils are automata to be built into computerised profiles – they can, if not used to excess, give balance in the overall coverage of observation throughout the school.

Some of these will be completely internal – say, a checklist of progress in reading: others will be local but arise from outside the school, such as checkups to be used in connection with the area mathematics guidelines, and others, such as Lindsay's *Infant Rating Scale* will be externally produced but allow flexibility in how and when the observations are carried out. Different forms of these structured devices are considered in Chapter 10.

Besides being consistent in what is observed, it is important also to be consistent in how it is reported. It is tempting to think that the word 'fluent' in a checklist on oral language has some objective reality, but clearly the 'fluent' of a fourth-year junior teacher will refer to a different performance from that of the teacher in charge of the reception class. Where numbers or letters are used in checklists or scales, it is even easier to fall into the 'equivalence' trap.

As any student will tell you, one man's A is another's C – and the same can apply in the primary school. Unless such gradations, whether expressed in short phrases such as 'Knows the concept' or in literal, numerical or tick-cross ways, are based on clearly observable criteria they will *not* be equivalent in the hands of different teachers, and unreliability will have been introduced into the assessment programme.[3]

Questioning

Teachers may be surprised to find a section on questions in a book about testing. Nevertheless, questioning gives a very direct and immediate form of feedback, whether applied to a class, group or individual. A variety of classifications of questions exists.[4] That presented below is designed solely for the purposes of this book and in the hope of encouraging teachers to think about this somewhat neglected area.

Functions of questions
As with other forms of assessment, questions can be used for baseline, ongoing or final (summative) purposes. At the beginning of a project, either by a class or an individual, it is helpful to assess what is known and what misunderstandings there are so that the level can be pitched appropriately and progress from the base-line measured. Ongoing information will be valuable as a guide to the state of the game: whether an explanation in mathematics is being followed, whether the major points of a discussion have been remembered, whether this week's talk can proceed on an adequate recall of last week's material. Summative information is perhaps less easy to obtain by oral means if a full picture of class level is required, but some suggestions are made in the section on internally produced tests.

Forms of question

RECALL QUESTIONS
These are likely to be the most frequently used, particularly when the request is for facts. 'Who can name one of Henry VIII's wives?'. They may be used in a variety of ways:

— to test immediate recall of *immediately* presented information. The teacher has told a story or given some information, and straight away asks questions about it.
— to test delayed recall of *recently* presented information. A typical situation is the recapitulation at the end of a lesson or discussion to test consolidation of the main points. Similarly, the teacher may wish to assess the remnants of last week's work before proceeding with the next stage.
— to test delayed recall of *more distant* information: 'I know from Miss Blackamore that you "did" the Tudors last year. Let's see what you remember about them.' – a form of revised base-line. Alternatively, at the end of a year, a teacher might get a feel for what her pupils recalled of earlier topics by a class discussion or quiz.

PROCESS QUESTIONS
Recall questions give a product, without telling much about the process in the child's mind which lead to that product. *Process*-type questions are aimed at getting on the inside of the child's thinking.

Sometimes these will directly address the child: 'Where did you get that from? What makes you think that's so?'

The answers: 'I worked it out for myself' (how?) or 'I heard it on the telly'. These represent quite different processes.

Others will be aimed at specific processes. Sometimes the teacher will be probing for a chain of operations which have already been taught: 'Explain to me how you would set about this one'.

Sometimes she will be looking for the ability to *generalise* beyond immediately presented examples, sometimes for *synthesis* of different skills or knowledge. The same question, 'How would you set about this one?' now assumes a different light: it is an invitation to the pupil to go beyond the information given and show his *own* reasoning powers.

Process questions can also be used *diagnostically:* when a child makes an error in computation, instead of simply showing the correct method, he may be asked 'How did you get that figure here?'. An interesting mathematical example is that of the child who consistently made errors like the following:

```
   24          36          39
 +  9        + 15        + 29
 ————        ————        ————
   29          49          59
```

When asked where all the nines came from, she replied 'Well, you said you couldn't have more than nine on the bottom line'. Teachers may thus learn something about their own processes of teaching as well as the thinking processes of their pupils!

Careful questioning
Much of the following section will be very familiar to the practised teacher. However, it is worthwhile reviewing some of the common dangers of questioning.

'One swallow doesn't make a summer'. The fact that one child understands is no indication that all do! Similarly, beware of the 'fallacy of composition'. You may have obtained correct answers to all your questions from different members of the class but this does not mean that all of the children know all the answers to all of your questions. You are not entitled to say, 'The class knew all I wanted them to know'.

Spread the questions. Most teachers are well aware of the need to assess progress 'at the back', but may be less aware that there tends to be a definite 'arc of fire' for each teacher where attention and questioning by the teacher are most concentrated.

Adjust the level of the questions. Whilst it is important to assess what children do not know as well as what they do, they should not be put in the position of never being able to expect success when answering questions. This poses a slight problem since, if easy questions are asked, able children may always answer them; if hard questions are asked, then slower children will become frustrated. Thus, it is not sufficient for the teacher to have the topic in mind whilst framing questions, but also to have in mind the range of ability, and indeed individual children's ability, so that she can check for different levels of recall or understanding.

Internally produced tests

According to this book teachers are actually testing in some form or other every day. This section, however, is concerned with more set-piece tests constructed within the school. Whilst these are common enough in secondary schools, they are far rarer in the primary range, for reasons which include the following:

- Contemporary emphasis is more on learning how to learn than simply on the acquisition of facts.
- Individualised activity rather than the lock-step of class lessons, especially in integrated studies, militates against a common test for all children, even in the same class.
- Competition is far less evident than 25 years ago, so that tests which deliberately order children against each other are not compatible with the more group-orientated and cooperative climate.
- Similarly, classification into streams or sets is unusual, again reducing the need for competitive-type tests.
- As noted in Chapter 3, there has been a general swing from norm-referenced to criterion-referenced tests in the last decade or so.

In spite of these arguments, some teachers may feel that they would like to have a measure of what has been learned as a result of a particular piece of educational endeavour – say, a topic in history. It may be felt that even where children have produced different themes, some common ground should be evident which will outlast the eventual consignment of the carefully produced folders to the rubbish bin.

It would be odd if one spent one's educational life learning how to learn, without anything specific having been learned as a result of this! Primary-age children, in the author's experience, positively enjoy quizzes (which is how such tests can be presented) provided they feel that no dire educational consequences depend on them.

The teacher has a number of choices in constructing such instruments. The first, general, one will be whether she wishes the test to cover objectives set at the outset or whether she is more interested in what the children have taken from a topic. The decision will depend partly on the subject matter. For instance, mathematics lends itself, perhaps wrongly, to the former, pre-objectives, approach, and history perhaps to a more open one. It will also depend on the teacher's view of her own role – whether as instructor or as facilitator of children's own learning.

Thus the question 'Name three of Henry VIII's wives' implies that the teacher has intended the children should reach this 'criterion' and, equally importantly, that she considers it *worthwhile* for them to have reached it. But if she asks 'What's the most interesting thing you have learned about Henry VIII?', she is adopting a more open attitude, probing for what *has* happened in children's minds rather than for what *ought* to have happened.

The detailed construction of objective tests is beyond the scope of this book, but the following general points can be made:

- One should use a simple 'content-process' model (see p. 21) to check that adequate coverage is given to each aspect to be assessed.

- In particular, consider what balance would be expected between knowledge and understanding.
- In testing understanding, is it understanding within the teaching material presented which should be tested, or the ability to generalise beyond to other areas?

Format of internal tests

A hypothetical example of different ways of presenting questions is given for consideration on p.70. Here, the following major issues can be outlined[5]:

1. *Essays.* These are not greatly in favour in primary schools, and there are many practical objections to their use as an accurate form of assessment. The subjective element is high, the time and length of marking stints have been shown to affect ratings, and handwriting has consistently exerted a 'halo' effect on the content. It also leaves the children, rather than the teacher, in control of what is produced.[6]

2. *Short-sentence answers.* Greater control can be exercised by the use of questions which require just a short sentence as the answer: the teacher is now sampling the children's learning for herself, rather than relying on what they offer.

3. *Single-word answers.* 'Open-completion' items can require single-word answers and thus avoid contaminating knowledge of the subject with linguistic ability – a further problem with essay-type formats.

4. *Multiple-choice tests.* These are, perhaps, the ultimate in control. Here the child *selects* rather than *produces* the responses. A large number of questions can be completed in a short time giving greater coverage of content than by any connected writing format. A word of warning: multiple-choice tests are apparently easy to construct (witness any woman's magazine questionnaire of love life) but they do, in fact, require much thought. Don't try one without reading about their construction first! It is often argued that they can only test knowlege, but this is far from so. Here is one example at the teacher's own level:

   If equal weights of ice at 0°C and water at 100°C are mixed without any gain or loss of heat to the surroundings, the resultant temperature would be:
   A   exactly 50°C.
   B   more than 50°C but less than 100°C.
   C   0°C.
   D   less than 50°C but more than 0°C.

A very different proposition from

The melting point of ice is:
A 32°C   B 0°F   C 32°F   D −32°F

5. *Quizzes*. Thoughts of content are likely to turn on the more obvious academic elements. But a good deal of background to what underpins children's understanding of their work can be obtained by taking more general themes not directly derived from school work. The author and his students derived great pleasure and interest from contructing simple quizzes to check on children's concepts of time – from simple, short-term questions such as, 'About how long did I hold my breath?' to longer-duration ones such as:

> Which of these happened since your mother was born?
>
> The first television
> The first motor car
> The first electric light
> The first photograph
> The Second World War
> The First World War
> The first man on the moon

Answers from young children can be very revealing, and somewhat embarrassing!

6. *The question of 'contamination'*. This has already been raised (see p.65). It is important that the format of the test does not prevent the child from showing what he *can* do in the area of interest to the teacher because he lacks other skills. An obvious example would be to give a written multiple-choice test to a poor reader: his knowledge and understanding is contaminated by his reading disability.

One way out of this is to use an oral presentation, asking children to write down either a number or an initial of the item of their choice. Even here, however, contamination may occur with young or slower children because of memory overload. It was a problem of contamination that caused the abandonment of the author's otherwise promising test of phonic skills. That test was in this format:

> Put each of the letters or groups of letters on the left with each of those on the right, and write down any real words that you find:
>
> | *tr* | *ane* |
> |------|-------|
> | *cr* | *ein* |
> | *r* | *ead* |

In spite of careful demonstrations, it was the *intellectual* ability of systematically running through the combinations that contaminated the actual phonic ability.

Notes

1 Southgate, V., *Extending Beginning Reading,* Heinemann, 1981. Chapter 10 gives a very full account of outside observations of what actually goes on in reading periods.

2 A good summary of the hazards affecting teachers' judgements of children is given in Downey, M. and Kelly, A.V., *Theory and Practice of Education,* Harper and Row, 1975, Chapter 1.

3 The interesting concept of 'triangulation', in which teachers can compare their accounts of what happened in the classroom with those of pupils and an observer was developed by the Ford Project. An account is available in Harlen, W., *Evaluation and the Teacher's Role,* Macmillan, 1978, Chapter by Elliott, J.

4 A very useful workbook on questions has been developed by the Teacher Education Project at the Universities of Leicester, Nottingham and Exeter: Teacher Education Project, *Effective Questioning and Explaining,* Macmillan, 1981.
   An example of the Ford Project's application to questions can be found in Hurlin, T., *Question Strategies: A Self Analysis,* Ford Teaching Project, 1975.
   An excellent practical analysis of discussion is in Sutton, C., *Communicating in the Classroom,* Hodder and Stoughton, 1981, Chapter 4.
   'Pre-determined' questioning is looked at closely in Barnes, D., *Language, the Learner and the School,* Penguin, 1969, Part One.

5 See Macintosh, H.G. and Morrison, R.B., *Objective Testing,* Hodder and Stoughton, 1969. Rae, G. and McPhillimy, W.N., *Learning in the Primary School,* Hodder and Stoughton, 1976. Although concerned with science and oriented towards the secondary school, the following short booklet gives an excellent introduction to the construction of items: Lyth, M., An *Item Writer's Handbook,* Hart-Davis, 1976.

6 Short practical advice on evaluation of project work is contained in a book devoted to primary school projects. Incidentally, it stresses the importance of enjoyment as a criterion! Waters, D., *Primary School Projects,* Heinemann, 1982, pp.59–62.

For further thought

1. At the end of a day, look back at the oral questions you have used and then try to categorise them into – for instance:
    Questions leading to predetermined answers;
    Questions leading to more open answers and discussion;
    Knowledge questions; and
    Process questions.
    Did you 'spray' the questions at the class or were some purpose-built for individual children?

2. If you are really brave, you can tape-record a discussion session (unobtrusively), and see what part your questioning played in it.

3. Look through the 'test' overleaf and consider how you might use the different items, or why you wouldn't:

Pleuterre

Pleuterre is a flat, largely swampy area of some 800 square miles lying immediately south of the Republic of Reignum, and separated from it by the barrier of the Levation mountains. Its coastline is about 40 miles long, the estuary of the Grand Bach cutting a gap of five miles into it.

The capital is Vivrici, which contains a third of the area's population of 16,000. The main industry is the processing in the capital of the shlerpin root, which grows abundantly around the curious stilt-like houses of the villagers, and is turned into the much-prized 'groviere'. The finished product is sent by flat-bottomed boat south down the estuary to Tieup, and thence by steamer to Europe.

The natives are a placid people, fond of water sports in the calm shallows of the swamps, and the rougher waters along the coastline. Because of the extreme humidity and the risk of malaria, it is unlikely their placidity will be troubled by European invasion or exploitation. The few white people who act as agents for the European importers seldom stay more than six months at a time.

A *Essay* Write a full account of what you know about Pleuterre.

B *Recall or open-completion*
   (a) What is the capital of Pleuterre?   ....
   (b) The capital of Pleuterre is   ....
   (c) The main industry of Pleuterre is the manufacture of ....
   from the .... This is carried out in the capital, ...
   (d) Map test (This would consist of a blank map to be filled in as required by the questions.)

C *True/False*
Tieup is the capital of Pleuterre.   ....

D *Multiple-choice*
   (a) The capital of Pleurre is:
       Levation   Tieup   Vivrici   Reignum   Groviere
   (b) The main industry of the area is:
       (i)   Building stilt-like houses
       (ii) Growing the shlerpin root
       (iii) The manufacture of groviere
   (c) Choose the most likely reason for the placid nature of the people of Pleuterre.
       (i)   Their stilt-like houses
       (ii) Their fondness for water sports ·
       (iii) Freedom from invasion because of risk of malaria
       (iv) The extreme humidity

(d) Rewrite the words on the left in the appropriate spaces on the right:

Vivrici   A root grown in Pleuterre   ....

Groviere   The mountains north of Pleuterre   ....

Grand Bach   The capital of Pleuterre   ....

Shlerpin   An edible product made in Pleuterre   ....

Levation   The main river of Pleuterre   ....

E *Rearrangement*

Place the following in order, from north to south:

Vivrici   (i)   ....

Reignum   (ii)   ....

Tieup   (iii)   ....

The Grand Bach Estuary   (iv)   ....

The Levation Mountains   (v)   ....

---

4. If the staff-room overlooks the playground, join with a colleague in observing one child for five minutes, and then compare your impressions. Did you use a 'general impression' method or look for particular behaviour? Did it matter whether you had had close contact with the child before?

For group discussion

1. Gather together a variety of children's project work and use it as a focus to compare teachers' different criteria for assessment (if any!). How much attention, for instance, is paid to presentation, content, the use of study skills, and to independent thought?

2. Compare reactions to the use of the various Pleuterre type questions for primary children.

3. Do you feel that the essay still has a place in primary assessment?

6

The Assessment of Reading

The function of reading in the curriculum of a primary school will vary with the age and stage of the children. Infants and their teachers will be much concerned with 'learning to read', whereas in the junior department, the emphasis is likely to be more and more on 'reading to learn' – on using reading as a tool of learning rather than as a skill in its own right. Thus any *single* test of reading is unlikely to be a perfect match to the objectives of the reading curriculum if used throughout the primary stage.

Reading taxonomies

In order to improve the match between testing and teaching, a *reading taxonomy* may be helpful. These vary from the detailed and elaborate Barrett's taxonomy, which breaks down the reading process into 23 sub-divisions[1], to the simple one devised by the classroom teacher to ensure that she is covering suitable objectives for her children, and to indicate what type of testing would be most appropriate for those objectives.

Although over-rigid adherence to a taxonomy may suggest that reading can be developed as a set of watertight skills practised in isolation, a broad division such as that suggested below may help to broaden perspectives on reading and thus on its assessment.

Word recognition skills: the ability to use visual and phonic information to 'decode' individual words.

Contextual skills: the ability to use clues derived from connected passages to supplement and support the information from individual words. These will include grammatical clues, meaning clues, knowledge of likely sequences of letters within words and of likely sequences of words within sentences.

Comprehension skills: These may be subdivided into three categories:
– Reading the lines: literal or explicit comprehension. The child can answer simple, direct questions by reference to the text as it stands.
– Reading between the lines: interpretive or implicit comprehension. This involves the ability to make inferences not directly stated in the text, but implicit in it. It may involve features such as predicting what will happen next or why someone behaved as they did, when these are not immediately apparent from the material.
– Reading beyond the lines: evaluation and appreciation. By this stage, the child can judge the appropriateness of a text for its purpose, distinguish emotive propaganda from fact and reason, and is developing a personal taste in his reading activities.

Information skills: These obviously overlap with the previous set, since we can hardly gain information from texts we don't understand. There are, however, some additional techniques – such as the ability to combine information from several sources (not necessarily all written), the ability to select books to suit information needs, and within books to locate desired information.

Even so crude and short a list of reading possibilities must surely throw doubt on the wisdom of using an individual test of word recognition, such as Schonell's, as a measure of reading at different ages and in its different aspects. Yet recent surveys have shown that such tests are still 'top of the pops' amongst primary schools[2], in spite of the availability of an increasing range of tests to suit different purposes.[3]

Selection of a published reading test

Individual oral test

Word recognition
If we are genuinely interested, as obviously many teachers are, in the word recognition level, then a test of 'words in isolation' may be appropriate (see Figure 6.1).
Such a test can give us an idea of a child's general level of reading – that is, it will correlate quite highly with other reading tests – but its use has two disadvantages: it does not give good information on any other aspect of reading, such as the use of context, and, if undue attention is paid to the results of such tests, they may bias the reading curriculum in favour

of the early skills. Indeed, it has been forcefully stated that the power to test reading is the power to determine the reading curriculum.

tree	little	milk	egg	book
school	sit	frog	playing	bun
flower	road	clock	train	light
picture	think	summer	people	something
dream	downstairs	biscuit	shepherd	thirsty
crowd	sandwich	beginning	postage	island
saucer	angel	ceiling	appeared	gnome
canary	attractive	imagine	nephew	gradually

Figure 6.1   From *Graded Word Reading Test,* A1, F.J. Schonell, Oliver and Boyd, 1945. A word is scored as correct if it is pronounced appropriately, whether or not it is understood.

Sentence reading
If we wish to go beyond the individual word, and allow the child the benefit of words in context, then a sentence reading test may be appropriate. In a typical oral test, the pupil reads a series of short sentences (see Figure 6.2) until he has made a certain number of errors.

1. Look at the book.

2. The sun is red.

3. He got some sweets from the shop.   6:2

4. We should not play football in the street.   6:6

5. The teacher wants to clean the blackboard.   6:10

6. She is watching the busy traffic speeding by her

   cottage.   7:2

Figure 6.2   From *Salford Sentence Reading Test,* Form C, G.E. Bookbinder, Hodder and Stoughton, 1976. The child reads until he has made a *total* of six errors. His reading age is given at the end of the line in which he makes his sixth error.

Whilst this clearly widens the range of reading beyond the pronunciation-without-comprehension of the individual word test, it still gives no guarantee of the child's understanding, since he may struggle through a sentence accurately but without comprehension. Thus we have not tested the *comprehension* level of our taxonomy.

Comprehension

Obviously, to test comprehension, questions will be needed. But here there is a dilemma: there are two possible sources of difficulty for the child now – one his inability to read the words accurately, and secondly his inability to understand or respond to the questions. The difficulty of a passage will thus depend partly on the difficulty of the questions.

We can divide questions very crudely into *explicit* types, which can be answered by direct reference to a passage, the answer appearing there in a clear form, and *implicit* types, where some rearrangement or rethinking is required before the answer can be achieved. Thus, the following sentence appears in a well-known history text on the Normans: 'There were no potatoes yet.'

An explicit question might be: 'Were there any potatoes in Norman times?'

An implicit one could be: 'Could you have had a chip butty then?'

The latter requires (beside a knowledge of chip butties!) at least a three-step process:

      (i)   What do we need for the butty? Chips.
      (ii) What do chips come from? Potatoes.
      (iii) Did the Normans have potatoes? No.

Therefore: (iv) Poor old Norman children couldn't have chip butties.

A series of explicit questions might produce a high score, whilst the use of implicit questions would probably lower it. Further, the bias of the type of question might once more bias the type of reading emphasised in schools. This may partly explain the Bullock Report's complaint about undue emphasis on 'literal' comprehension in the teaching of English.

A test which tries to disentangle the 'mechanical' and 'understanding' aspects of reading is Neale's *Analysis of Reading Ability*. There are three parallel forms, each containing six passages of ascending difficulty. The pupil reads each passage aloud, having been told there will be questions on it, and is then asked a series of laid-down questions (see Figure 6.3).

The tester notes errors, and can , if she wishes, record these in the diagnostic framework suggested by Neale. Testing continues until a prescribed number of errors is made or exceeded in a passage. From the number an accuracy score can be found, and from the number of questions right, a comprehension score can be obtained – thus

A robin hopped up to my window.

I gave her some bread.

She made a nest in my garden.

Now I look after her little birds.

Figure 6.3   From *Neale Analysis of Reading Ability,* Form C, M.D. Neale, Macmillan, 1958.

1 ROBIN (26)	Mis*	Sub	Ref	Add	Oms	Rev
A						
robin						
hopped						
up						
to						
my						
window.						
I						
gave						
her						
some						
bread.						
She						
made						
a						

1 continued	Mis	Sub	Ref	Add	Oms	Rev
nest						
in						
my						
garden.						
Now						
I						
look						
after						
her						
little						
birds.						

Errors ....

Time ....

Comprehension ....

Questions
1. Where was the little boy/girl standing when the robin hopped up to him/her?
2. What did the little boy/girl give the robin?
3. What did the robin do in the garden?
4. How does the little boy/girl help the robin now?

*Key to diagnostic categories: Mispronunciation, Substitution, Refusal, Addition, Omission, Reversal.

comparison of the two abilities and the identification of the child with undue problems in one as compared with the other. In order to avoid confusing problems of accuracy with those of comprehension, the tester may prompt on any word where the child hesitates for four seconds or more. Thus the gist of the passage is not lost because of the failure to read a word, though the omission counts as an error.

Group tests with written responses

In the examples given so far, the child has read aloud to the teacher or tester. They are, therefore, individually administered tests of oral reading. The same aspects of reading can also be tested using written responses, and in a group situation.

Word recognition
The children indicate on their papers which of a group of five or six words corresponds to a picture or to a word given in a sentence by the teacher (see Figure 6.5).
   This, of course, is not quite the same as reading an individual word aloud. Sometimes the right word, though unknown to the child, can be found by the elimination of alternatives, and, as with all multiple-choice tests, there will be the problem of the lucky guess – though this will normally have been allowed for in the scoring procedure.

Sentence reading
Until recently, by far the most frequent group test of reading has been the sentence-completion type. In this, the child selects from a group the word which best completes a sentence (see Figure 6.4). This has an advantage over the orally-read sentence test, in that the child must understand the sentence before he can select the appropriate word (although informed guesses will, of course, occur).

---

19.   Thunder makes a loud <u>noise</u>   <u>news</u>   <u>nose</u>   <u>nice</u>   <u>nest.</u>

20.   String is used to tie up a <u>pickle</u>   <u>parcel</u>   <u>park</u>   <u>poem</u>   <u>pull.</u>

21.   The policeman stopped the <u>toffees</u>   <u>today</u>   <u>time</u>   <u>terrific</u>   <u>traffic.</u>

22.   I bounce a <u>bell</u>   <u>boat</u>   <u>doll</u>   <u>bun</u>   <u>ball.</u>

Figure 6.4   From *Southgate Group Reading Test 2,* Form B, V. Southgate, Hodder and Stoughton, 1962.

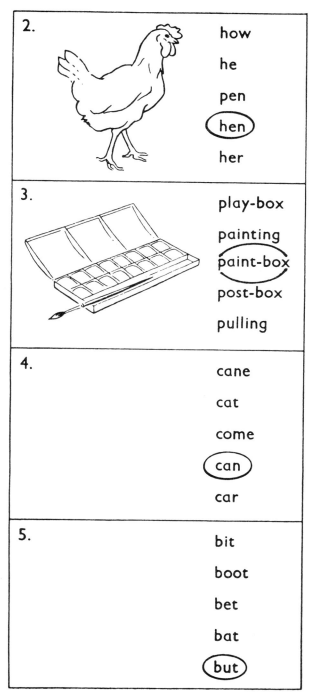

2. how
   he
   pen
   (hen)
   her

3. play-box
   painting
   (paint-box)
   post-box
   pulling

4. cane
   cat
   come
   (can)
   car

5. bit
   boot
   bet
   bat
   (but)

Figure 6.5   From *Southgate Group Reading Test 1*, Form B, V. Southgate, Hodder and Stoughton, 1962.

Such tests can also include a disguised vocabulary element, in that the child may be able to read a word mechanically, but be unaware of its meaning. Indeed, Daniels and Diack, in writing of their own *Standard Test of Reading No 12,* have said that reading ages of over ten years should be viewed with caution because of their reliance on vocabulary.

Tests of this sort are common, and are available from the infant stage (e.g., the *Southgate Group Test 2)* to the secondary stage (e.g., *NFER Reading Test EH, No. 1).* They have formed the basis of estimates of national abilities in reading *(Test NS6* and the *Watts-Vernon Test),* but have been heavily criticised by the Bullock Report: 'We do not regard these tests as adequate measures of reading ability. What they measure is a narrow aspect of silent reading comprehension.'[4]

What, then, can be done to select test material which does not merit such criticism? One answer is to use a compendium of tests, preferably derived from the same source to avoid problems of comparison and combination. A recent and popular example is the previously-mentioned *Edinburgh Reading Tests.* These will enable the teacher to sample her pupils' reading abilities in a systematic way which will give both a general impression of reading development and more specific information on sub-skills such as reading for facts, comprehension, retention of main ideas, points of view, and vocabulary.

Such tests also go some way towards meeting another criticism of the traditional sentence-completion test – that it is a highly artificial situation, far removed from the purposes of reading in everyday life. By the use of illustrations, advertisements, recipes, the test can be made more relevant to real life than, say, 35 unrelated and possibly sterile sentences.

It should be pointed out, however, that just because a test has several sections, it does not follow that it can give specific information on different aspects of reading. Spooncer's *Group Reading Assessment,* for instance, has three separate sections, but these are all intended to work towards a reliable assessment of accuracy in reading and do not give three separate measures. Once more, the manual should be read to establish what the constructor's intentions were.

The 'cloze' procedure
It is difficult to categorise the cloze technique as testing a particular facet of reading since, at its best, it can cover so many. Essentially, it consists of a passage from which words have been deleted so that the child has to fill the gaps. The argument is that he will bring a range of skills – perceptual, syntactical and comprehension – to bear on this, so that the testing is done in a way in which the reader *naturally* brings his orchestrated abilities to bear on predicting what will come next.

Although its use has only become frequent recently, it dates back at least to the *Kingston Test* of 1954. A number of methods of deletion are possible. Sometimes small 'functor' words like *in, an, on,* are removed, it being assumed that the child will not be able to fill these in appropriately unless he has correctly read the remaining words. Sometimes content words will be removed.

The advantage of removing small words is that the child will be unlikely to have spelling problems with them, and the advantage of having the child construct rather than select a response lies in the elimination of guessing. Some tests, such as McLeod's *GAP* test do not penalise for wrong spelling; Spooncer's *Group Literacy Assessment* does require correct spelling in Part 2, since it is deliberately designed to include spelling in its compass.

A very recent addition to published cloze tests is Young's *Cloze Reading Tests,* which offer three levels from second-year to first-year secondary, using mainly the small-word approach which lessens spelling problems (see Figure 6.6).

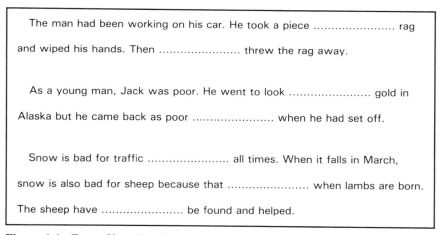

The man had been working on his car. He took a piece .... rag

and wiped his hands. Then .... threw the rag away.

As a young man, Jack was poor. He went to look .... gold in

Alaska but he came back as poor .... when he had set off.

Snow is bad for traffic .... all times. When it falls in March,

snow is also bad for sheep because that .... when lambs are born.

The sheep have .... be found and helped.

Figure 6.6   From *Cloze Reading Tests,* Level 3, D. Young, Hodder and Stoughton, 1982.

Individual or group?

The general arguments relevant to individual or group testing have been considered in Chapter 4. In reading, the use of a single, non-consumable test-card may be very appealing on grounds of cost but may be very time consuming in practice. Where a single test, such as the *Salford Reading Tests,* may be helpful is in the testing of a pupil new to the school, or in the confirmation of the results of a group test.

One danger in the use of individual reading tests is over-subjectivity by the tester. The author has often played tape-recordings of Schonell Tests to teachers, and invited them to score them. The results show that the same recordings, played on the same occasion, can result in variations of at least a year in reading age.

It is important to drop the role of teacher when acting as a tester, and to take a more neutral and objective attitude. It has been well claimed that standardised tests are a notably successful attempt to restrict unreliability – and it would be a pity to throw this advantage away by over-sympathetic testing.

Descriptive or diagnostic?

Sometimes a straightforward summary of what has been achieved so far – the stage of reporting introduced in Chapter 2 – will be all that is required: at the beginning of a year, an attainment test will facilitate grouping and the provision of appropriate materials. At the end, it will provide a basis for reports to other teachers and to parents. But, since reading is so complex a process, it will also be more necessary than in any other aspect of the curriculum to go beyond the purely descriptive stage to a more detailed diagnosis. This in turn will form the basis for a programme designed to improve the reader's performance in any areas found to be weak. A typical testing cycle would then be:

- attainment testing: the descriptive level;
- diagnostic testing: the diagnostic level;
- programme development: the prescriptive level;
- progress testing: and so on.

The main forms of reading attainment tests have been described above. The diagnostic tests available may concentrate on a single aspect – such as the *Swansea Test of Phonic Skills* (1972) – or they may form part of a compendium or battery such as the *Standard Reading Tests* of Daniels and Diack (1958). In either case, the teacher can gain help on the prescriptive aspect since specific advice may be given on what to do to combat weaknesses.

Thus, Jackson's very detailed *PS Tests of Phonic Skills* (1971), 11 in all, also provide suggestions for developing individual remedial programmes, and both the Standard Battery and the very useful West Sussex *Assessment of Reading Ability* (1972) provide follow-up suggestions in the light of the test results obtained.

Reading age or standardised score?

Statistical argument distinctly favours the standardised score as a method of reporting results. But in reading particularly, primary teachers are perhaps happier with the concept of an attainment age. This figure compares the performance of an individual child with that of a typical child of the age stated, so that a child of a chronological age of ten years but with a reading age of seven has performed at the level of a typical seven-year-old.

A reading age provides a convenient anchor in that the teacher will know which books can be appropriately given to children of different reading ages, and will also have an idea of what types of reading skills are likely to have been acquired by children of a given reading age. In other words, it will serve as a kind of criterion reference in a way that the standardised score cannot.

Against the use of a reading age is the fact that any test, such as Burt's *Word Reading Test* (1974 Revision), which is used across a wide age range cannot have a normal distribution across the range: at the lower end it may exhibit the floor effect, and at the top may have too low a ceiling. Further, a reading age of, say, nine years obtained by a seven-year-old and by a 12-year-old are quantitatively the same – but qualitatively may be quite different. It would, for instance, be quite foolish to design similar programmes for the two pupils simply because they had achieved the same reading age. The standardised score would show very clearly the considerable difference in standing relative to the respective peer groups. Such criticisms apply less to the narrow-band test which is purpose built for a particular age group.

It is important not to become confused between a *reading quotient,* derived in the past by the formula

$$\frac{\text{reading age}}{\text{chronological age}} \times 100$$

and a *standardised reading score,* derived by the methods described in Chapter 2. They do not yield equivalent results, and serious misconceptions can arise if they are alternated indiscriminately. As an example, a score of 59 on Level 2 of Young's *Cloze Tests* gives a reading age of 14.0 years, and a standard score of 124 for a child of exactly ten years. Yet the application of the traditional quotient formula gives a reading quotient of $\frac{14}{10} \times 100 = 140$. The author's advice is to use reading ages or standardised scores as seems appropriate but to avoid the use of the older formula.

The consequences of using either a reading age or a standardised score when selecting children for remedial help are important. If the reading age is used, it will act as an 'absolute' measure, and, generally speaking, will throw up more young children (in Britain, those born in the summer term) than older. This fact is well attested by many surveys. On the other hand, if the standardised score is used, it will tend to produce – since it contains an age allowance – an even spread across the age range. The school must, therefore, decide whether it wishes to go for criterion referencing, i.e. helping all children below a certain reading age, whatever their chronological age, or to go for norm referencing, i.e., helping all children who have a similar standing relative to their age group, whatever their reading age.

Internal sources

The advantages of internal assessment procedures for reading are, of course, similar to those in any other area of the curriculum, but with the added attraction that, unlike many skills, reading can be monitored as it is going on, particularly in the early stages. The teacher is thus in a position to assess and redirect immediately, rather than having to wait for the completion of a process (such as writing a story) before reviewing the product.

For the maximum advantage to be obtained, it is important that the teacher should be systematic in her procedures, and avoid the possible sources of bias indicated in Chapter 5. One teacher, for instance, might tend always to assess accuracy in reading, omitting to check on understanding. Different teachers might have different standards as to what they would consider an acceptable reading of the same text. Once more, a simple taxonomy, whether borrowed or devised by the teacher, will help to provide appropriate coverage in assessment.

Hearing children read

One of the simplest sources of internal assessment, particularly in the infant and lower junior stages, is that of hearing children read. This simple, everyday, situation can be used to provide many of the different kinds of information given by external tests – subject, of course, to the reservation that it is taken from the standpoint of the particular teacher involved.

Attainment can be gauged in terms of progress through a scheme (or level in a colour-coded programme). For grouping purposes, *normative* comparisons can be made ('Where does he stand in relation to the rest?') and so can the criterion 'Is he ready for the next book? Has he passed the criteria I consider prerequisite for moving on?'. *Progress* can be considered thus: 'How long has he taken to get through this book? Should I be looking for something easier, or does he need to be advanced a little?'.

Miscue analysis

The diagnostic aspect of hearing children read can be deepened by the use of miscue analysis.[5] Goodman used the term to avoid the unfortunate connotation of words like 'wrong'. He believed that the *observed* response which the child makes in place of the *expected* response derives from the same basic processes as correct reading: 'In comparing unexpected responses in oral reading to expected responses, the ... reading process is revealed.' Miscue analysis thus opens a window on the related reading processes of the use of grapho-phonic, syntactic and semantic information.

Goodman's original taxomony of miscues has 28 divisions, which may be far more than the classroom teacher would wish to use. The process can, however, be used with a much simpler set of divisions, depending on the level of the pupils and the intentions of the teacher. At early levels and in remedial work, teachers may wish to concentrate on 'mechanical' problems, such as visual confusions, reversals and inability to apply phonic rules.

At later levels it would be well to remember Goodman's advice that reading is a process of acquiring meaning, not one of 'recoding' from a visual system to a sound system. The author thus uses a rather broad set of miscue categories, closely adhering to the following description by Goodman of the three parallel reading processes:

Visual miscues: Substitutions of words or letters of similar appearance; reversals of words or parts of words; omissions which suggest inadequate word attack.

Phonic miscues: Substitution of incorrect phonic interpretation, e.g., 'met' for 'meat'.

Syntactic miscues: Insertion or substitution of words which violate reasonable syntactic expectations (e.g., 'She collected a *beautiful* of eggs' for 'She collected a *basketful* of eggs').

Semantic miscues: Insertions or substitutions which suggest inability to understand the message of the text (e.g., 'He *shouted* him the moon' for 'He *showed* him the moon').

It is important to remember that all these miscues may interact, so that a visual miscue may lead to a change in subsequent 'predictions', with the child drifting further and further off course. Goodman suggests that where a miscue does not lead to corruption or loss of meaning, it is relatively unimportant, but clearly where a child is miscuing so often as to make comprehension difficult, some remedial help is advisable.

In this connection, it may be helpful to distinguish between *habitual* errors, which are typical of the child's performance, and *occasional* which may have been triggered off only by the particular passage being read. A distinction between *unreasonable* miscues, which produce words violating sight, sound, syntactic and semantic clues, and *reasonable* or 'virtuous' miscues, which are utilising at least part of the information available, may also assist in distinguishing important from unimportant erors.

In a strict miscue analysis, the teacher may play the part of a tester, not assisting the child, in order to see more clearly the latter's individual reading process and problems. In everyday work, however, the teacher can combine the roles of tester and teacher, noting the errors made but also helping the child towards correcting them – not necessarily by prompting but by asking why he said a certain word and what might have been a better response. In this way, both teacher and child are learning together, the one about his pupil, and the other about reading.

No amount of miscue analysis, however detailed the taxonomy and careful the technique will be of long-lasting value without some system of recording errors. The hard-pressed teacher cannot carry in her head the performances of 30 children, so some form of record is essential. This should certainly go beyond the simple card which records the page the child has reached, but its detail will depend on the purposes for which it will be used. Ideally, of course, the descriptive material of the analysis should provide the basis for later work (see Figure 6.7).

The great advantage of miscue analysis is that it presents an entirely flexible, and immediately responsive, set of tools for the diagnosis of the reading process. It should be remembered, however, that in reading to teacher the child is giving a performance, as it were, and may, as Elizabeth Goodacre points out, feel the need to maintain output – in other words the performance heard by the teacher might not be identical with that of the child when reading at his own table.

Comprehension

Miscue analysis does give some idea of whether the child is understanding what he reads, but a more systematic assessment can be gained by asking definite questions, either whilst hearing him read or at the end of a story or book. These questions should be matched to the level of the child: some children will only be able to cope with the explicit question, the answer to which is already on the page, whilst others will be able to read between the lines with ease. Questions can of course also be asked at the evaluative and appreciative levels – 'Which story did you like best? Why was that?'[6]

Criterion information

Hearing children read presents an ideal situation for criterion analysis since, essentially, it brings together the teacher's knowledge of the

Sentence to be read	Error category	Method of recording error	Example
Which is the way to the house on the hill?	Substitution	Underline the word misread and write in word substituted	'home' Which is the way to the house on the hill?
	No response	If the child *waits* to be prompted or asks for a word, underline with a dashed line	Which is the way to the house on the hill?
	Addition	Use caret mark and write down word or part-word added	'go to' Which is the way to the house on the hill?
	Omission*	Where words are omitted, circle them	Which is the way to the (house) on the hill?
	Self-correction	Where errors are self-corrected, record by using initials 'S.C.' over the words	S.C. Which is the way to the house on the hill?
	Repetition	Record word/s repeated by putting 'R' over appropriate section.	R Which is the way to the house on the hill?
	Mispronunciations	Indicate where stress is placed	Which is the way to the house on the hill?
	Ignores punctuation	Circle punctuation ignored	Which is the way to the house on the hill?......
	Reversals	This is a form of substitution, but may be of diagnostic significance if part of a regular pattern	'no' Which is the way to the house on the hill?

* Child does not wait for help.

Figure 6.7 Coding for recording error types. From *Reading: Tests and Assessment Techniques*, P.D. Pumfrey, Hodder and Stoughton, 1976.

skills of reading and the child's progress through them. This aspect has been formalised in the construction of a set of reading levels which can help to match material to learner. They can be described as:

Frustration level: Useless to the child: he can do little with it and is largely wasting his time.

Instruction level: The child can benefit from instruction by the teacher: he can cope for much of the time, but needs some help.

Independent level: The child needs little help: the material is easy for him, so he can consolidate his already learned skills.

Formal criteria for these levels have been set as follows:

Frustration: More than 10% of words are misread or not attempted. Comprehension is low: tension and withdrawal from the task are obvious.

Instruction: Not more than one error in 20 words. After silent study, the passage is read in a conversational tone with proper phrasing and lack of tension. The majority of the material is understood.

Independent: Not more than one error in 100 words. Comprehension is almost complete. Well-phrased reading with freedom from tension.

Two points should be noted in using these levels: frustration in either accuracy or comprehension is damaging to the child, and the level of comprehension shown will depend on the nature of the questions asked.

Cloze procedure

The teacher can use this technique in a number of ways.[7] It will give her a general idea of the reading strategies used by her class, since it will in effect be a kind of group miscue analysis, and it can also be used to gauge the level of reading material appropriate to the individuals within it. This can be done by preparing a set of cloze passages, graded in difficulty, from materials to be used with the class. Whilst the same match can be attempted by the use of a published test, this method has the advantage of using the actual texts that the children will read.

Alternatively, as Pumfrey (1976) suggests, the child can read a series of complete passages from the class materials arranged in order of difficulty, and the level of each child can be found as indicated on page 88. Also, perhaps a miscue analysis can be done, as described above. The group cloze procedure has the advantage of giving quick information. The individual naturally demands more of a teacher's time but can give greater depth of feedback.

The informal reading inventory

This is really a systematic recording of what the teacher discovers about each child's reading. It can be very flexible, content and design being adapted to the needs of a particular teacher and her class. A possible outline might be:

Attitude to reading: Confident/interested/reluctant/defeated.

Interests in reading: Type of stories preferred.
Any non-fiction interests.
Use of libraries.
(The above information could be gathered either from individual interviews, incidental obser-vations, or the use of a simple pupil questionnaire for older children.)[8]

Level of reading: – Described by the results of a published test, giv-ing name and date.

– Described by the level within the reading scheme or materials which seems most suited to the pupil: ascertained by cloze procedure, graded passages read orally, or for older pupils graded passages with written comprehension questions.

– For the information skills the teacher can de-vise tasks requiring the use of a table of con-tents, an index, the finding of facts within a single passage or book, or the choosing of a suit-able book for part of a project from the library. (See the section on the work of the APU, p.91.

Screening

In reading, screening is likely to be used to detect children who are 'at risk', and who therefore require extra help in order to avoid becoming failing readers in the secondary school and perhaps in adult life.[9] As with other areas, there will inevitably be hits and misses, and these will occur whether a 'home-grown' set of instruments is used or a published version. The typical procedure involves the administration of a group reading test, the isolation of a group for further investigation by individual attainment, and more importantly, diagnostic, tests.

Thus, the Barking Project (Buckley, 1978) used a 'retardation' of 24 months in the first year of junior school (a common time for screening) which threw up about 12% of all pupils as being possibly at risk. Further investigation was carried out using a series of diagnostic tests.

The immediate results of the Barking 'action research' – involving the development of programmes of remedial help which could be selectively applied to any individual according to the diagnostic results – were very promising. A total of ninety three selected 'at-risk' children improved by an average 23.5 months in the first eight months of the project, whilst seven 'control' children (otherwise similar in status) improved by only 10.7 months.

Against this optimistic outlook, a follow-up in the West Riding six years after the initial screening revealed a large number of misses: three quarters of those needing later help by the School Psychological Service were missed by the screening (Rennie, 1980). It is important, therefore, not to regard the screening as a one-off device but to support it – for instance by later teacher observations. Children may have had a lucky streak of guesses on a multiple-choice group test, some who coped at the early stages of reading may have lost motivation later, some may have had unfortunate educational experiences such as frequent changes of teachers.

It is unreasonable to expect any test to forecast with complete accuracy what will happen six years later, and it is foolish to act as if it could do so. In considering screening, we can ask a number of questions:

1. At what age is it wished to screen?

2. How will the target 'at-risk' group be identified?

    – Standardised score below a certain figure (see p. 56)
    – As the lowest percentage of the year group?
    – From the gap between chronological age and reading age?

3. What tests will be set
(a) for the initial screening, and
(b) for the diagnostic follow-up?

4. Who will be involved? Class teachers, the school psychological service? How and when?

5. What is to be done about the results?
(a) Are the results to be merely distributed for information to teachers and schools?
(b) Are specific suggestions for help to be made? If so, how and by whom?

6. What monitoring of progress will be used
(a) to check on the progress of the 'at-risk' group, and
(b) to check on the misses, i.e. the children who escaped the early net.

The work of the APU

The APU (see Chapter 1, p.10) has paid considerable attention to the Bullock Report's desire for real-life tasks to test reading, and has devised a series of such tasks based on booklets containing passages about, for instance, whales. The material was prepared as a collaborative exercise between Unit members and teachers, the content being selected from books 'of a kind likely to be employed or referred to by teachers of 11-year old children' (the age at which children are tested at the primary level).

In each booklet there are about 2,000 words to be scanned, skimmed or read in detail, and the pupil has to answer questions requiring skills such as:

– locating information within a sentence, a paragraph or several paragraphs;
– relating information between different passages;
– the use of an index to find an appropriate passage for given information;
– evaluating, e.g. for the 'Whales' booklet: 'Having read through this booklet, can you think of any reasons why whale-killing should be stopped? (Base your answer on the information in the pamphlet, but you are welcome to use your own ideas too).'

Whilst the booklets have been criticised for not being really life-like, they can provide the stimulus for the construction of internal assessments, particularly on the information skills, and on evaluating and appreciating.[10]

Notes

1   The framework of the Barrett taxonomy is given in Pumfrey, P.D.,
    Measuring Reading Abilities, Hodder and Stoughton, 1977, Chapter 8.
    A fuller treatment is in Open University, Reading Development,
    Course PE 231.
    A starting point for the development of a classification could be Hunter,
    E., *Reading Skills: A Systematic Approach,* CET, 1977.

2   The general picture seems to be that while *authorities* have moved away
    from tests involving the reading of isolated words, schools still continue
    to use them: See, Friend, P., 'The use of reading tests in primary
    schools', *Reading,* Vol.15, 1981, pp.15–20; O'Donnell, D.H., 'Assess-
    ment within schools: a study in one county', *Educational Research,* 1981,
    Vol. 24, No. 1; Wood, R. and Gipps, C., 'The testing of reading in
    LEAs: the Bullock Report 7 years on', *Educational Studies,* 1981, Vol.
    7, No. 2.

3   Information about reading tests, and appraisals of them, can be obtained
    from: Pumfrey, P.D., *Reading: Tests and Assessment Techniques,* Hod-
    der and Stoughton, 1976; Turner, J., *The Assessment of Reading Skills,*
    UKRA, 1972; West Sussex County Council, *Assessment of Reading
    Ability.* A short, but very valuable, introduction to reading assessment,
    periodically updated, is Latham, W. and Overall, L., *Assessment Pro-
    cedures in the Teaching of Reading,* Sheffield City Polytechnic Language
    Development Centre.
    More general consideration is given in: Pumfrey, P.D., *Measuring Read-
    ing Abilities,* Hodder and Stoughton, 1977; Raggett, M.StJ., Tutt, C.
    and Raggett, P., *Assessment and Testing of Reading,* Ward Lock, 1979;
    Vincent, D. and Cresswell, M., *Reading Tests in the Classroom,* NFER,
    1976.

4   Bullock, Sir A., *A Language for Life,* NFER, 1976, Chapter 2.

5   Miscue analysis and 'Hearing children read' are treated in: Goodacre,
    E., *Hearing Children Read,* Centre for the Teaching of Reading, Uni-
    versity of Reading, 1972; Goodman, K., 'Analysis of oral reading mis-
    cues' in Smith, F., *Psycholinguistics and Reading,* Holt, Rinehart and
    Winston, 1973.
    The journal *Reading* (UKRA) freqently contains practical articles on
    the diagnostic hearing of children's reading, such as: Campbell, R.,
    1981, Vol.15, pp.26–32; Hartley, D., 1981, Vol.15, pp.37–40; Lamb, C.,
    1981, Vol.15, No. 1; Potter, F.N., 1981, Vol. 15, pp.21–6.

6   Different levels of question corresponding to different levels of com-
    prehension are illustrated in Melnik, A. and Merritt, J., *The Reading
    Curriculum,* Hodder and Stoughton, 1972.
    'Reading the lines', 'Between the lines' and 'Beyond the lines' are put
    into practical context in a series of textbooks: *Scope for Reading,*
    Holmes McDougall, 1979. The 'information' skills can be developed
    and informally assessed by consulting Cooper, J., *Directions: Reading
    Skills,* Oliver and Boyd, 1978.

7   Walker, C., *Reading Development and Extension,* Ward Lock, 1974.

8   For help in the construction of an informal reading inventory see: Open University, Reading Development, Course PE 231; Pumfrey, P.D., *Measuring Reading Abilities,* Hodder and Stoughton, 1977, pp.154–60.

9   Buckley, M., *et al.,* 'Barking at Bullock – Reading screening: Barking's integrated approach' in Hunter-Grundin, E. and H.U., *Reading: Implementing the Bullock Report,* UKRA, 1978. The Bullock Report shows how screening is applied in practice in Chapter 17, which also contains notes on hearing children read, the informal reading inventory and the frequency of test use in schools.
     A cautionary note on screening is sounded by Rennie, E., 'The West Riding screening six years on', *Educational Research,* November 1980.
     Practical accounts of screening and the use of checklists can again be found in journals, such as: Bailey, J. and Rogers, C., 'An infant reading check', *Association of Educational Psychologists' Journal,* 1979, Vol.5, No. 1; Blagg, N.R. and Lawrence, D., 'The Somerset Developmental Checklist', Remedial Education, 1982, Vol.17, No. 3.
     A particularly comprehensive breakdown in skills into the four areas of listening, speaking, reading and writing, covering the range from infant to middle school, is *Take it as read,* Blandford Teachers' Centre, Dorset Education Committee.

10   The work of the APU: DES, *Language Performance in Schools,* Primary Survey Report No. 1, HMSO, 1981; Report No. 2, HMSO, 1982.
     It is worth looking at these two reports in full, so that you can assess the type of material used for yourself. They are, however, summarised in DES/APU Summary Reports Nos. 4 and 10.
     The approach of the APU to language assessment is heavily attacked by Rosen, H., *The Language Monitors,* Tinga Tinga, 1982.

Test Bibliography

Bookbinder, G.E., *Salford Sentence Reading Tests,* Hodder and Stoughton, 1975.
Hebron, M.E., *Kingston Test of Silent Reading,* Harrap, 1954.
McLeod, J., *GAP Reading Comprehension Test,* Heinemann, 1970.
Neale, M.D., *Neale Analaysis of Reading Ability,* Macmillan, 1958.
Jackson, S., *Phonic Skills (P.S.) Tests,* Robert Gibson, 1971.
Schonnell, F.J., *Graded Word Reading Test R1,* Oliver and Boyd, 1942.
Southgate, V., *Southgate Group Reading Tests 1 and 2,* Hodder and Stoughton, 1959, 1962.
Spooncer, F., *Group Literacy Assessment,* Hodder and Stoughton, 1981.
Williams, P., *Swansea Test of Phonic Skills,* Blackwell, 1972.
Young, D., *Cloze Reading Tests,* Hodder and Stoughton, 1982.

For further thought

1. What published reading tests are in use in the school, and for what purpose? Are the most relevant tests being used to assess reading objectives?
2. When you listen to a child reading, do you just mark the page and any difficult words on the bookmark? Of course not. What *do* you do?
3. Make a list of the skills that you think of as 'information' skills and devise situations which would assess them.
4. Tape-record a child while he is reading aloud without helping or correcting him – but explain to him why help is not being given! Then go through the tape (a) by yourself, trying to analyse and record the miscues, and (b) with the child, getting *him* to point out any errors and why he thinks he made them.

For group discussion

1. A tape-recording is made of a child reading from, say, Schonell's *Graded Word Reading Test*. Each member of the group should record the errors they notice. The group can then compare the number and type of errors recorded by different listeners.
2. A tape recording is made of a few children reading the same passage, some fluently, some haltingly. Listeners should then classify the reading as being at 'frustration', 'instruction' or 'independent' level (p.88); they should also note whether they would change the book. Compare the results.
3. Construct a series of questions on a piece of 'information' material; they should cover explicit or literal comprehension, implicit comprehension and evaluation. Discuss the questions.

7

The Assessment of Written Work

The teaching and testing of reading has been almost a national obsession over the past 20 years or so, but the assessment of written work in the primary school has received rather less attention, apart from vague complaints about falling standards. One reason for this may be that in writing, other than dictation, there is no pre-existing 'correct' version against which the pupil's response can be checked. Writing is a productive activity, the nature of which cannot be predicted completely, and it is therefore least amenable to external assessment by those who do not have a personal knowledge of the writer and his intentions.

Dimensions of written work

One of the most important dimensions of written material is that between its *surface* and *deeper* qualities. Surface qualities include punctuation, spelling and grammatical accuracy. These can thus be assessed against some prescribed standard – either a spelling is right or it is wrong. These formal aspects are thus temptingly easy to judge, but over-concentration on them may reduce attention to the deeper aspects of communication, such as aspects of style, the appropriateness of style to purpose, the use of imagery and the expression of feelings. Indeed the National Association of Teachers of English writes baldly:

> Spelling, punctuation, synonyms, grammatical analysis and grammatical correctness are only indirectly connected with the main purpose of expressing or understanding feelings, attitudes and ideas. (Stibbs, 1979)

Clearly, then, the teacher must decide what her attitude is towards these two dimensions, both in the long-term planning of her curriculum and in the short-term assessment of written work.

Where the task set is a formal one – say in the use of speech marks – the requirements of the teacher will be clear to the children, and the exercise can be quite straightforwardly assessed. But where the situation is more general – as in writing a story – both specification of objectives and criteria for assessment are likely to be far less clear. Studies over the last half-century or more have consistently shown how the same essay can be quite differently rated by different markers: in other words, unless great care is taken, the unreliability in the assessment of written work is likely to be high.

Whilst published tests can be helpful in testing of the surface aspects – a number of spelling and general English tests are described later – they cannot offer more than guidelines to the more general assessment of writing.

Writer and audience

Writing is intended to be an act of communication, and in communication there is a *communicator* who sends a *message* to an *audience* with a certain *purpose*.

The communicator in the classroom is easy to establish: it is the child. Identification of the audience is less easy. Theoretically, a wide range is possible. The child may write only for himself – notes, a poem, a story, for his eyes alone. He could write for others in the school – an account of the district football final for a school meeting. He could write for an audience outside the school – either a particular person, such as the chairman of the local Council protesting against large lorries endangering the roads near school, or to the public at large, as in an appeal for help with material for a local history project.

In the practical world of the classroom, it is likely that there is in fact one definite audience: the teacher. Even if the child is writing along the lines suggested above, more often than not the work will be received, marked and vetted by the teacher, and the child will be conscious of this from the outset. It is thus very important how the child views the teacher. Possible roles in which the teacher may be cast (often quite differently for different children in the class) might be as:

– a sympathetic and trusted adult;
– an objective and professional helper;
– an examiner.

The child's willingness to risk ambitious failures – of spelling or style – is likely to decrease from the first to the third of these viewpoints. 'I'll be judge, I'll be jury', said cunning old Fury, 'I'll try you severely and condemn you to death' – this is not likely to motivate the child towards exposing himself. He may thus write not what he thinks, but what he thinks teacher thinks he ought to think – and this game is played right through from primary school to university.

Process or product?

When the teacher 'takes the books in' she is receiving a tangible *product*. But the story, the project work, are of course the result of a *process*. In terms of assessment, therefore, the teacher, besides asking 'What have the children done?' must also ask 'What has this done to the children?' In other words, her objectives must be concerned not only with the production of material, but with the beneficial changes in the ways in which her pupils think and express themselves.

The processes involved in writing are similar to those in any form of productive activity. The work can be *reproductive* – in an extreme form, simple copying – or *recreative,* as in a cabin's boy's view of the Battle of Trafalgar. There will be degrees of *expressive* activity, where the intention is to communicate or express for oneself feelings and attitudes, and there will be genuinely *creative* processes, where the pupil brings something new to the product.

Douglas Barnes distinguishes between 'transmission' and 'interpretation' views of language.[1] The first of these is closer to the 'reproductive' side of the divisions above, since attention is focussed on the product, as a sign that the pupil has acquired and adequately recorded certain information. The 'interpretation' aspect is more concerned with the process, with pupils having to reinterpret and evaluate knowledge and events before making it their own in the act of expression.

It will be seen that there is some similarity with the reading taxonomy of the previous chapter: the reproductive and transmission categories parallel literal comprehension, rendering unto Caesar that which is Caesar's, whilst the interpretative and expressive/creative aspects are more like reading between the lines and reading beyond the lines. We could summarise thus:

Writing the lines: accurately recording existing information

Writing between the lines: reinterpreting and re-organising information and experience before committing it to the written form.

Writing beyond the lines: Combining information, adding one's personal viewpoint, feelings and attitudes to form an integrated and balanced piece of personal writing.

Purpose: teacher's or pupil's?

The degree of teacher control is an important dimension in writing. We have seen that in more formal aspects, teacher and pupil may be well in accord that, for example, 'we are practising punctuation.' Outside these more formal aspects, however, the degree of control may vary considerably.

A class writing about an old man, for instance, might be told 'I want you to bring him to life for me – write about his looks, his clothes, how he moves, where he lives, who he meets'. Here the class have been given a virtual blueprint for their descriptive activities. But if McTell's 'Have you seen an old man who roams the streets of London?' is played as a stimulus, and they are invited to describe how they would feel, old and alone in a big city, the degrees of constraint are apparently much less.

Class discussion may, nevertheless, still provide a blueprint due to the comments of the teacher (to have 40 country lanes 'dappled with patches of bright sunlight' is a clear warning against over-enthusiastic reception of children's phrases) and there will be a further, hidden, blueprint: the class's knowledge of what teacher likes, as exhibited by her spoken and written comments and methods of correction.

The teacher must, therefore, decide whether she has definite expectations from a piece of writing and, if so, whether she has made these explicit to her pupils, or whether she is willing to assess the work in terms of the purposes of each individual – that one child may write a narrative story about an old man, another concentrate on description, a third use it as an introduction to more general comments about old age.

She will also have to decide, and again make clear to the children, where she is concentrating on surface features, and where she will be considering deeper aspects. Her task is not an easy one: Harpin, in *The Second R* writes:

> Assessment is a considered response to a piece of writing taking account of its purpose, its intended audience, the situation of the writer and his writing history, leading to suggestions for more effective realisations of the thoughts, feelings, information, arguments that the writer is trying to express.[2]

– a tall order, to which we will now turn.

Assessment of written work

Published tests

Spelling

Perhaps because of its black-and-white nature (it's either right or wrong!), spelling is well represented in publishers' catalogues.[3]

Although it has been argued that spelling is best treated by criterion referencing ('What can he spell? What does he need to learn to spell?') rather than by normative referencing, both categories are available.

Schonell's early and still relevant work included separate tests of regular and irregular words, together with a set of graded dictation passages which can be used either for initial placement in his teaching material (*The Essential Spelling Lists*) or for assessment of progress. Thus there is, as in reading, both the assessment of success with words in isolation and with words in context and a rather tight relationship between test and teaching material.

Both Schonell and Daniels and Diack, who include a spelling list of 40 words in their *Standard Battery* (Test 11, 1977), offer some simple diagnostic suggestions. Schonell suggests the teacher looks for these types of confusion:

> *visual:*   *agian* for *again, brigth* for *bright;*
> *auditory:*   *agane* for *again;* and
> *major:*   *acar* for *again, folne* for *foreign.*

Daniels and Diack give the first two categories, with a fourth, that of spelling irregular words in a phonetically regular way (e.g., *dun* for *done*).

Peters (1975) has constructed three diagnostic dictation passages for junior-age children which can be analysed into five classifications for given indications of the child's problems. In particular, errors can be described as:

- reasonable phonic alternatives, (readable in the light of the passage) e.g., *cote* for *coat*);
- phonic alternatives not conforming to normal spelling precedent (e.g., *suacer* for *saucer*); and
- random words (e.g., *ctanc* for ?????).

Examples of errors are given for each passage.

Where applicability over a wide age range is desired, Vernon's *Graded Word Spelling Test* (1977) may be suitable. A different band of words is suggested for different age groups, and spelling ages from 5.7 to 15.10 months are given, with standard scores from 5.6 to 17.6 years, though with some qualification at the lower end since different schools will have different policies as to when and how to begin spelling. No diagnostic suggestions are made, and Vernon is clearly wedded to the virtues of a 'systematic' rather than an 'incidental' approach.

The spelling section of Young's *Spelling and Reading (SPAR) Tests* can also be used over a wide range, quotients (but not spelling ages) being given over the range 7.0 to 15.11 months. Instead of using different bands of the test, however, the teacher is able to make up to ten entirely different but equivalent tests from the 'item banks' provided. Thus, problems of practice effects are minimised, and the material can be used to chart progress over a number of years.

For teachers who believe in the early detection of problems, Marie Clay's dictation test in *The Early Detection of Reading Difficulties* gives a score based on the accuracy of phonemes (sound units) within words, and a diagnostic set of categories including acceptable alternatives (*skool* for *school*), sequencing errors, the omission of sounds and unusual placement of letters.

General
The NFER (see Chapter 1, p.10) offers in particular a series of tests covering both primary and secondary stages. They are labelled as *English Progress Tests,* and typically contain items relating to spelling, punctuation, vocabulary and comprehension, together with grammatical competence.

They can thus be used to obtain base-line data on the formal aspects of written English – for instance, at the start of a school year or as a check on the more informal assessment of the teacher. They provide normative rather than criterion data but are not designed by the same constructors, have not been standardised on similar populations, and several were originally produced in the 1960s or earlier.

The *Richmond Battery*, besides testing reading, also has sections on usage, punctuation and spelling, and therefore can also be used where a formal assessment of surface features is required.

Internal assessment

Spelling
As indicated above, some writers and teachers believe in the systematic teaching of spelling – that it is 'taught' rather than 'caught'. For these, the use of a published test with its normative implications that certain words will be learned at certain ages, will harmonise with their teaching approach. For those who believe in a more incidental approach – that the most satisfactory source of spelling teaching lies in the actual words needed by children in their written work, that spellings should not be taught in isolation, and that undue attention to spelling inhibits spontaneity of writing – such a test is likely to be meaningless.

In fact, both the 'systematic' and the 'incidental' teacher are in a strong position to monitor their pupil's progress without necessarily having recourse to a published test. The more formal teacher will often use a spelling list, such as Schonell's *Essential Spelling Lists,* and can use selected words from the list both as teaching and testing material ('Learn these ready for a test on Friday'). She will, of course, be using several different lists appropriate to the range of spelling ability in the class, since this is a form of 'mastery' learning: the criterion is that the children shall succeed, not fail miserably.

Alternatively, she may have noted common errors and interest words during the week, and base her material on these. Again what *must* be avoided is giving the same test to the whole class, or giving one in which low marks are frequent.

The actual mechanics of administering several tests at the same time are quite simple. If each group is given an initial, the teacher can say,: 'Group A: sausage. Write "sausage" (putting the word in a sentence if ambiguity is likely)'. Whilst Group A struggle with their sausage, she says 'Group B: rabbit', and so on. Vernon recommends that the children use separate *printed* letters and is cautious about pupils correcting each other's work.

The teacher who believes in a more individual approach can also keep careful account of progress and problems. As described later, there will be ample opportunity to observe and help with errors in written work, and she may also have the evidence of the child's word-book in which she will write words requested by him. These can be used for individual checks to ensure that the child is not passively receiving teacher's help but actively trying to learn the words.

An interesting suggestion made by Marie Clay, and which can give useful baseline data on young children, is to ask them to write 'all the words they know' for ten minutes. For older children, though, Clay does not suggest this. They may be asked to 'write the 30 hardest words you think you can spell correctly'. In either case, the children are given a chance of exhibiting what they can do, not what they cannot do, by means of a self-administered rather than externally imposed test.

General

MEDIAN SAMPLES

The nearest thing to a published test of connected writing is the median sample technique.[4] This was used over half a century ago by Sir Cyril Burt in assessing the written abilities of London children, and was taken up by Schonell in his *Backwardness in the Basic Subjects*. A series of topics is given to the children, who write without guidance or discussion. The pieces of writing are arranged in order of quality, for each age group, and the middle or 'median' one is taken as representative of the typical writing abilities of that age.

Burt used 'My home' as a topic, but Schonell widened the range to include:

Narrative-descriptive: 'My school';
Imaginative: 'If I had wings and could fly';

Explanatory: 'How to play... (a game chosen by the child)'.

By comparing any child's work on these topics with the age scale of median samples, a kind of written-work age can be obtained – but since both the titles and standardisation are somewhat out of date, the teacher may wish to adapt the method for her own purposes.

At the beginning of a year, it is helpful to obtain base-line data on children's writing, and if topics are given which are likely to sample different types of language – informative, expressive, as the teacher decides – the teacher will have a sample of her children's present abilities on which to base her future work. But how is she to assess this sample?

IMPRESSION AND ANALYSIS

Two major methods of assessment are the *impression* and the *analytic*. In the first, the work is read as a whole, though the impression may be guided by implicit or explicit criteria; in the second, a definite marking schedule is adopted with different weight sometimes being given to different aspects. Burt suggested that attention should be given to:

The more mechanical aspects: writing, spelling, punctuation, grammar and syntax.

The more literary aspects: range, correctness and appropriateness of information, vocabulary and 'rhetorical devices'.

The logical aspects: organisation of ideas, complexity, relevance, sequence of sentences and paragraphs.

Much more recently, Crystal (e.g., in Stubbs, 1979) has suggested:

Technical features: spelling, punctuation, grammar.
Content: Selection and connection.
Organisation: Structure, consistency and layout.

It has been suggested that, whilst more systematic, the analytic method may fail to capture the overall feel of the work.

Since the use of actual marks (7/10) is infrequent in the primary school, it is unlikely that teachers will want to use the analytic method to obtain a numerical grading. However, a simple taxonomy on the lines of those above will ensure that the teacher thinks about her criteria for assessment, so that she does not fall into a rut of expectations which the children will quickly discern.

The criteria need not, of course, always be the same for different types of writing: some topics may lend themselves to organisation, others to the use of good vocabulary and style. What should be avoided is confining attention to the surface or technical aspects. This, in turn, is likely to result from a negative rather than positive attitude to assessment.

Burt advised: 'The common method of marking compositions – to ignore positive excellencies, to note only definite faults.....is almost worthless from a scientific standpoint'. This view is repeated again and again. Harpin, for instance, suggests: 'Reinforce what is good, look for and praise facets of growth and development, *before* attending to difficulties'.

Feedback on written work

As we have seen, the actual audience for most written work is the teacher, and therefore feedback will most often be from teacher to child. This undoubtedly subtle process can be divided into a few major aspects: it can be *oral* or it can be *written*. The written form is permanent, likely to be shorter, and possibly more impersonal than the oral.

'What a lovely idea! Just try to avoid too many bad spellings next time, will you?', spoken quietly, is very different from the peremptory 'Too many careless errors' as the child's reward for his labours.

Feedback can be *specific* or *general*. Specific comments can be made on particular points, which will include the use of good vocabulary, striking images, and the technical features such as spelling and punctuation. Studies of the methods actually used by teachers to comment on or correct individual points in the same story show a tremendous variation in feedback techniques. In the treatment of misspellings, for instance, some teachers simply indicate the error, others write in the whole word correctly, others modify only the incorrect letters (see Figure 7.1).

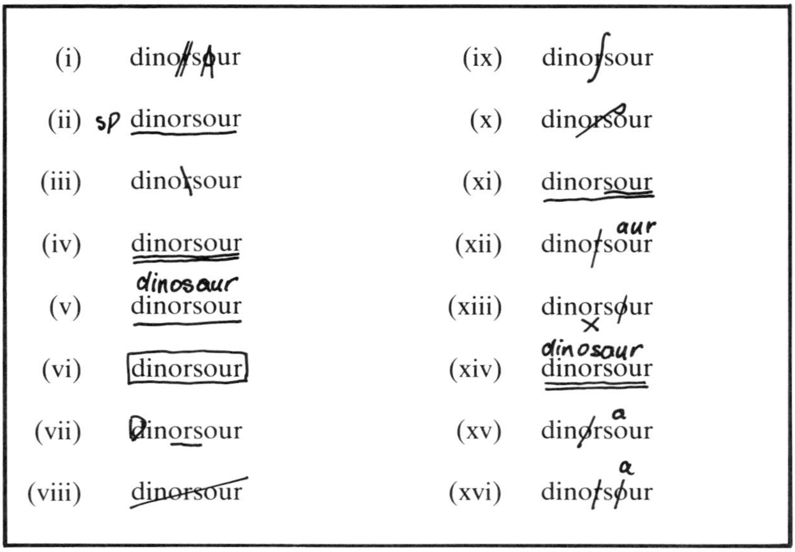

Figure 7.1   Ways of correcting a misspelling. From *Mark My Words,* T. Dunsbee and T. Ford, Ward Lock, 1980.

Feedback of the general sort, usually at the end, also varies greatly, as shown by different teachers' methods of commenting on the same story. Styles may vary, from 'Spelling atrocious. Go through this work and put it in the past tense. Do your spelling corrections. Very poor work.' (successive comments to the same pupil) to 'You explain your plans well and are self-critical in a constructive way in the last section'.

The teacher's summary comments will convey a definite attitude to the child, and may arouse strong feelings, as shown by pupils' reactions to correction of their work, for example: 'When I get a piece of work back and I think it is good and I get a bad mark, I feel like frotilling the teacher.'

In assessing an individual piece of work, the teacher will have to decide what particular features she will be looking for; what the balance between specific and general comments should be; how these will be conveyed to the pupil and, though it is outside the scope of this book, what advice on correction and development she will give. Because of the variety of approaches, it is no bad thing for teachers to look at work from other classes, and compare notes on what they admire and deprecate with their colleagues – and occasionally the views of the children on what they appreciate in each other's work might be salutary!

The work of the APU

The following list of the dimensions of writing proposed by the APU (see Chapter 1, p . 10) has much in common with those described above:[5]

Narrative – Descriptive or Reflective – Analytical
Controlled by writer or by tester
First-hand or second-hand subject matter (i.e. involving personal experience or knowledge derived from elsewhere.)
Literary or functional (i.e. story, or writing which informs or persuades)

In practical terms, these produce a set of seven categories of task for 11-year-olds, varying from stories and autobiographical narratives to accounts of how the pupil would carry out a task or project. In turn, these would be written in different contexts – i.e. with different audiences in mind. Thus:

Context A: Writing produced in traditional test conditions.
Context B: Produced in response to a specific task on a given occasion

by a teacher to whom the pupil is accustomed to address writing.

Context C: Pieces selected by the teacher from writing produced in the normal course of classroom work.

The Unit is very conscious of the point made earlier, that whatever imaginary audience is proposed, the child is likely to be aware that his work will be seen by an adult appraiser. The method of evaluation used involved both impression and analytic elements, and in commenting on the merits of these it was pointed out that impression marking may be biassed by interest in one or two specific aspects of writing, whereas with analytic marking, the overall feel of the piece may be lost. The impression marking was thus done on a scale from one to seven by *two* markers.

The dimensions of the analytic approach were: content and organisation; grammatical conventions and knowledge of orthographic conventions; and appropriateness and style. Scaled scores on impression marking had a correlation of 0.79 with knowledge of orthographic conventions, and of 0.88 with the assessment of content and organisation, suggesting that somewhat similar facets were being measured by both approaches.

Notes

1 Barnes, D., *Language, the Learner and the School,* Penguin, 1969; Barnes, D., *From Communication to Curriculum,* Penguin, 1975.
2 Harpin, W., *The Second R,* Unwin, 1976.
3 *Spelling:* Clay, M., *The Early Detection of Reading Difficulties,* Macmillan, 1981; Daniels, J.C. and Diack, H., Standard Reading Tests, Test 11, Chatto and Windus, 1958; Peters, M.L., *Diagnostic and Remedial Spelling Manual,* Macmillan, 1975; Schonell, F.J., *Backwardness in the Basic Subjects,* Oliver and Boyd, 1942; Schonell, F.J., *Essentials in Teaching and Testing Spelling,* Macmillan, 1932; Vernon, P.E., *Graded Word Spelling Test,* Hodder and Stoughton, 1977; Young, D., *SPAR (Spelling and Reading Tests),* Hodder and Stoughton, 1976.
   A recent addition to the assessment of spelling, criterion-referenced and including a questionnaire on attitude to spelling is Vincent, D., and Claydon, J., *Diagnostic Spelling Test,* NFER-Nelson, 1982.
4 The 'Median Sample' method is described in Schonell, F.J., *Backwardness in the Basic Subjects,* Oliver and Boyd, 1942; Burt, C., *Mental and Scholastic Tests,* Staples, 1962.
   For the 'reception' of children's work the following include excellent practical illustrations and exercises: Dunsbee, T. and Ford, T., *Mark My Words,* Ward Lock, 1980; Stibbs, A., *Assessing Children's Language,* Ward Lock, 1979; Stubbs, M., *Observing Classroom Language,* Course P232, Open University; Sutton, C., *Communicating in the Classroom,* Hodder and Stoughton, 1981.

For a very detailed taxonomy, illustrated by a wealth of examples, see Wilkinson, A., *Assessing Language Development,* Oxford University Press, 1980.

5   The work of the APU: (DES), *Language Performance in Schools,* Primary Report No. 1, HMSO, 1981; Report No. 2, HMSO, 1982. Though both of these are somewhat technical in places, they offer a wide range of illustration. They are summarised in the APU Reports 4 and 10.

A very critical analysis is again made by Rosen, H., *The Language Monitors,* Tinga Tinga, 1982.

A short follow-up to the Bullock Report gives a more sympathetic account of the APU's work: Department of Education and Science, *Bullock Revisited,* HMSO, 1982. It includes the information that when asked to 'improve' other children's work, pupils concentrated on .... spelling!

For further thought

1. When assessing children's writing, are you an examiner, a professional observer, a sympathetic friend? Or a judge, or a murderer? All things to all children?

2. List the criteria which are at the back of your mind when you read children's work. How far do these relate to surface, and how far to deeper qualities? Do your criteria vary with the age of the child or the type of material?

3. How would you categorise the different kinds of writing that your children do? (I.e. make a do-it-yourself taxonomy)

For group discussion

1. Photostat four pieces of writing done on the same topic by children of the same age. The group has to give an overall rating on a five-point scale, and then to 'mark' the work as they would in their own class. At the end, compare the ratings and the methods of marking and commenting.

2. Type out five pieces of work on the same topic, correcting any misspellings and poor grammar. Ask one group to rank them in order of merit, and to justify their choice. A second group should be given photostat copies of the originals, and again should rank these, justifying their choices. The two groups then come together to compare the rankings and the kind of justifications made.

8

The Assessment of Mathematics

Compared with the rigid mathematics curriculum of pre-war days, characterised by computation and so-called problems (we really did fill and empty baths with vast quantities of water, if not enthusiasm), the primary classroom today presents a considerable, if not bewildering, variety of approaches.

Topics such as set theory and topology, once thought to belong to much later stages of education, have been introduced. Mathematics is taught as not only contributing to life but as arising from and running through life. It is integrated with other areas rather than taught in splendid isolation, yet is also considered as a form of knowledge in its own right which can be sincerely taught and enjoyed in the primary stage.

Within this maze of change, guidelines proliferate, yet even so detailed a set as the *Nuffield Project* advocates 'bespoke' rather than 'off-the-peg' formulation of each school's curriculum. Thus no packaged deal exists, and the combination of internal and external assessment becomes a delicate, if not a paradoxical, matter.

Mathematical aims and objectives

As with other areas, it is perhaps easier to formulate general aims in mathematics than to proceed to clearly defined objectives.[1] Thus, a recent local authority guideline summarises its aims quite fairly thus: 'We teach mathematics because of its value as a subject in its own right, which can be enjoyed; because of its value as a "service" subject for other areas of the curriculum; and because of its use in everyday life.'

So far, so good. How do we translate this into a working pattern both for curriculum development and its consequent assessment?

Content

One way of ensuring coverage of the curriculum both in approach and assessment would seem to be classification by content. But content in mathematics is far more diverse than in, say, reading. Rightly or wrongly, we usually categorise reading into that of fiction and non-fiction, but in mathematics, even at primary level, we are dealing with a welter of topics: addition, subtraction, multiplication, division, fractions, weight, volume, ratio, percentage and so on.

Is there any way we can reduce these to a manageable set of main divisions? The popular Manchester guidelines use three main divisions:

Measurement: Money, time, weight, length, area, capacity and volume.
Shape: Shape and visual representation.
Structure: Sets, numbers and operations.

An apparently different set was produced during the NFER project *Assessment for transition;* when, after their list had reached 20 areas, they settled for:

Numbers: addition, subtraction, multiplication, division.
Properties of operations: shapes, ratio and proportion, money.

This was, however, for the special purpose of ensuring some comparability between the information passed from primary to secondary school.

To some extent differences in classification will reflect the commitment of the school or teacher to a flavour of mathematics teaching. The real-life, pragmatic, school will highlight those topics having a direct pay-off in everyday matters, or indeed in examinations. Those favouring maths-as-reasoning as a form of study in its own right may give priority to areas with less tangible pay-offs, such as the basic operations lying behind the number system.

To the real-life adherent, the study of different number bases might be justified by its contemporary application in calculators and computers in the form of the binary and hex systems; to the more theoretically inclined, their value might be in freeing children from the rigid confines of the denary system and encouraging them to think what a number system actually *is* rather than how it is used.

Fortunately, there are now available many guidelines amongst which schools can shop around for what suits their own purposes. Most of these guidelines are not imposed from above, but result from long and careful deliberations by teachers and other educationalists. There is, however, one danger in resorting to already available material: terms which are used in a particular sense in one guideline may not be appreciated in that way by an outsider who does not take the trouble to understand their usage. Thus, the simple term *addition* may conjure up to a teacher of infants 'Knowledge of addition facts to 10'. But to the Nuffield group, addition is

> An abstract operation performed on abstract numbers: it is defined in terms of the cardinal numbers of sets which have no common elements. For example if two such sets have the cardinal numbers 3 and 4 respectively, then the cardinal number of their union, namely 7, is the result of adding the cardinal numbers of their original sets, 3 and 4.

These are not merely terminological differences. They will affect the way the teacher assesses her children's number development.

The 'Let's-get-the-facts-right' teacher will look for just that, and perhaps nothing more. The 'understanding' teacher will be looking also for evidence that the child is operating the number system with some realisation of its basic principles. Similar divisions will occur between those who favour a more traditional approach, and those who include aspects of the so-called 'modern maths.' In their assessment procedures, they will be devising and looking for instruments which cover these aspects. This is important in the selection of external material, since it would be foolish to assess children by the use of a traditionally-loaded test, if the school's objectives are far wider.

Processes

The term *processes* is used here not in the sense of processes such as addition and subtraction, but in terms of what is going on in the child's head – in other words, they are psychological processes. The most basic division of these is that into *knowledge* and *understanding* – a division probably nowhere more apparent than in mathematics. Accurate computation can be achieved, as many of us know, without any real awareness of the principles behind our manipulations; but equally it is possible to have an understanding of basic principles without full knowledge of the nuts and bolts of the number system – as if we fully understood the working of the internal combustion engine, but had no idea how to drive.

At an early stage, the child, as a result of much practice, may be able to say that two and three make five. He may also 'know' that three and two make five. But he may not be immediately aware that three and two are the same as two and three – in other words, he cannot operate the commutative rule that elements in addition may be combined in any order. Such learning by rote and by rule can continue to secondary school, where some of us learned to 'solve' quadratic equations by the use of the formula:

$$x = \frac{-b \pm \sqrt{b^2 - 4ac}}{2a}$$

But does this *really* show understanding of quadratic equations?

Teachers may well protest that this is a caricature of modern teaching, that of course they teach understanding. In practice there is an obvious tension between the two, with schools varying in the emphasis they put on each. But we must be careful about what we mean by 'understanding'. In *Mathematics and the Primary School Curriculum*, Choat says 'skill should not be confused with understanding. Skill is the ability to carry out a set routine... and (may) be performed with relational or instrumental understanding'.[2] Many basic skills show only instrumental understanding, the ability to carry out specific operations in a sequential order by approved methods. Also, many children are adept in selecting the right set of processes, given a problem of a type they have encountered before.

Relational understanding, on the other hand, is not only knowing *what* to do, but *why* – it includes a knowledge of underlying mathematical relationships and properties. At its worst, instrumental understanding is a form of conditioned response; at its best it can only generate a set of uncoordinated techniques which cannot approach the beauty and significance of mathematics itself. It is as if one driver knew a set route to the Tower of London, and was lost if he deviated from it, whilst another understood the geographical relationships of the area, and could use a set of flexible, interrelated plans to reach his chosen end.

We must also remember that although mathematics, especially when viewed as instrumental understanding, may seem a highly convergent subject, it is also, largely through the work of Miss Biggs, taught as an area to be explored rather than passively received.[3] Some taxonomies of mathematics indeed include *inventiveness* in their categories, and we must therefore remember to include more open types of assessment which allow the child to do what *he* wants to do with mathematics, rather than always asking him to do what teacher wants him to do.

Internal assessment and mathematics

Probably no other subject is more continuously and conscientiously checked than mathematics. Many teachers would be ashamed if yesterday's work were unmarked before today's began. Ticks and crosses abound, checklists and record books are filled in, and a vast amount of data can be collected. As with reading, the process can be checked as the child is doing it, and, even more precisely than in reading, the teacher will be aware of what objectives she intends for the child. It would be a pity not to use so favourable a situation to its best advantage.

Sitting by Sid

The assessment of a child's work in mathematics as it proceeds is rather like that of hearing a child read. It can offer *attainment* information: what he can do, what page he has reached, what processes he has understood. It can offer *diagnostic* information. It offers great scope for *criterion reference* particularly where objectives are clearly known, and it can offer *feedback* to the teacher about her own teaching. Summarised onto a checklist or other records, these brief encounters can form the basis for *summative* assessment at the end of a term or year. Diagnostically, if we encounter an error we can:

(a) put a cross and let the child try to correct – very unhelpful;

(b) explain what has gone wrong – helpful towards instrumental understanding;

(c) Ask 'How did you get this bit?' – helpful diagnostically and in terms of the child's active rather than passive understanding.

Teacher-made tests

Generally speaking, these are less used in primary schools nowadays. There is, however, some value in teachers trying their hands at producing simple tests in mathematics. In mathematics especially, objectivity is often possible, and the act of constructing items can tell teachers a lot about their own thinking and about possible misconceptions by pupils. They may then see where difficulties arise other than from the mathematics itself.

   Poor reading is an obvious hindrance, unconnected with the subject. Less obvious, however, will be the effect of unfamiliar vocabulary and unfamiliar settings – as in this example from the Schools Council project, *Mathematics and the Ten-year-old,* in which the following two questions were put to comparable groups of primary children:

(a) | 0 | 6 | 2 | 9 | 9 |

What is the next number this meter will show? Write it in here.

Percentage right: 41

(b) The milometer on a car shows 06299 miles. What will it show after the car has gone one more mile?

Percentage right: 48

Some factor in the second question – more familiar setting or layout – seems to have made it rather easier.[4]

Internal tests can be used for a number of assessment purposes. Baseline data can be obtained from the administration of a short test, perhaps drawn up with the collaboration of the children's previous teacher, and this will corroborate the information in the ongoing record passed up from the earlier year (since we know that the summer holidays produce some loss in most children).

If the test is designed to have a diagnostic function (e.g., includes items on which children are known to have specific difficulties) it can be a further guide to future work and, if kept in a folder, can easily be referred to to check on progress and see what still needs to be done. The author's own advice would be to avoid normative interpretation of such tests, since the problems of combining and comparing marks from internal tests on a small sample are considerable. They should rather be regarded as criterion-referenced – as indicating the 'current mastery' of the child and what he still needs to master.

Teachers will no doubt think first of the 'constructive' type of item, in which the answer is left for the child to provide. Diagnostic information can, however, be obtained by the use of a selective format. Question (a) above, for instance, gave rise to the following wrong answers by the children:

07300   1731010   07299.

You might like to think of possible reasons for these errors. Where a pattern of errors in a process is known, the teacher can then construct a multiple-choice item incorporating them. Thus, we could change the format of question (a) to

What is the next number that this meter will show?
(a) 07300   (b) 1731010   (c) 06300   (d) 07299.

The advantage of such a format is that the teacher knows at once how many children have each type of misunderstanding, instead of having to run through all papers listing the problems. The disadvantage is that unless the distractors are plausible and meaningful, children may guess the right answer by elimination.

Such tests can also be used at the end of a year, as a guide to the teacher as to what has been retained by the children from the year's work. This may show some differences from the ongoing record, since topics studied early and not returned to may be less secure than expected.

When constructing internal tests, the following three points (over and above the general ones of Chapter 4) should be borne in mind:

1. Be clear on what is being tested – in content, in understanding (instrumental or relational?), and in knowledge.

2. Be clear why it is being tested – is it for baseline data, as a summing up, for progress, or diagnostically?

3. Be sure that irrelevant areas are not being tested – vocabulary, (other than mathematical), familiarity or unfamiliarity of situations, and, of course, reading.

Internal-external cooperation

Checkups

The work of Piaget has included and given rise to much exploration of concepts such as classification, seriation, conservation, identity and reversibility, which are fundamental to mathematical operations. Whilst teachers, especially in the infant school, will have much informal opportunity to observe the child's grasp of these in action, they may well wish to have somewhat more structured situations available. An extensive set is provided by the Nuffield Checkups which, without binding the teacher to specific apparatus, offer ideas for checking on the milestones of a child's conceptual development.

As the accompanying guides point out, they should not be taken as the sole evidence – they are there to confirm observations the teacher has made in daily work. They should not, therefore, be used as tests to be taken out with ceremony but as situations which simply extend the normal classroom procedure. They should also *certainly not* be used as guides to a curriculum or syllabus.

The whole essence of the approach is that children acquire concepts by their own activity, not by being told. The teacher is not helping the child's mathematical development by drilling him in these situations: they confirm, but do not produce, the existence of a concept. The situations may be very simple, as in this example from *Checking Up I:*

Material: One piece of long, narrow ribbon, dark grey.
           One piece of short, wide ribbon which should be light grey.
Ask: Are these two pieces of ribbon the same?
           How are they different?

A set of sample replies is given which indicates the child's transition from using a single relation ('That one's big, and that one's small') through successive comparisons ('That one's long, that one's short,' followed by 'That one's a darker grey than that one') to dual comparison ('That one's longer but narrower than that one' followed by 'And that one's darker grey') to the final simultaneous comparison of the three attributes.[5]

The teacher thus has a set of criteria against which to judge development, and she also has some warning signs about what can and cannot safely be attempted next. A child who cannot easily compare two dimensions simultaneously *may* be able to 'do' area sums by rule ('Multiply length by breadth'). But such an ability is only a low form of instrumental understanding, resting on what Piaget himself has called a 'conceptual vacuum'. The child is skating on thin ice, and may drown in bewilderment if repeatedly taken beyond his level of development. In a sense, these Checkups are 'readiness' tests – not in the way that reading readiness tests check on the child's preparation for beginning the whole process, but for his readiness to take the next step.

It must be admitted that the situations devised by Piaget, and incorporated into the guides, have been criticised in recent years, notably by Margaret Donaldson.[6] The authors of the Checkups themselves point out that children's responses may depend on the kind of material presented and the Checkups should not, therefore, be used blindly, but should be presented in the least ambiguous way that the teacher can devise without distorting their original purpose.

These particular Checkups are associated with one general approach. Many guidelines offer checkpoints – sometimes rather loosely attached to curriculum objectives, sometimes in the form of a 'question bank', to which we may now turn.

Question and item banks

The hard-pressed teacher may find it difficult to produce the range of items and situations necessary to cover her objectives. If she is using a definite book or scheme, it can of course be argued that the activity is its own assessment: if children are working through with accuracy and understanding, all is well, and the teachers's part is to watch for difficulties and help the children over them. But where a looser system operates, 'guides to the guides' may be helpful.

These give *examples* of suitable questions for assessing whether the relevant objectives of the main guidelines have been achieved, thus giving feedback to the teacher on the child's progress. It is important, however, to realise that such questions are illustrative rather than definitive: if teachers teach to them we are back to the straitjacket of assessment dominating teaching.

Such *question banks* can be general, or more precise, but do not have the statistical properties of facility and discrimination indices attached to them, since they have probably not been tried out systematically on large numbers. Where items have been so tried out, and their levels of facility and discrimination are known, they form an *item bank*. Such banks can form a powerful tool in both the normative and criterion assessment of pupils.[7]

The advantages of item banks include the following:

1. Items can be combined to produce an assessment instrument which is purpose-built for the objectives in mind. The school or authority does not have to buy a package-deal test which may fit only poorly with their intended objectives.

2. Because their statistics are known, items can be combined to produce a more rational scale than would be obtained by putting together untried questions.

3. Backwash effects can be minimised. If it is known that a test of a certain kind will be used, say at the end of the year, there is an inevitable tendency to 'teach to the test'. If monitoring by light sampling is used, then different items from different areas can be given to different children, thereby preserving the 'security' of the items from over-frequent exposure.

4. In all, therefore, it can be claimed that – by making use of item banks – schools and authorities are obtaining the rigour of external sources without their rigidity.

External sources

From the arguments of the preceding sections, it can be seen that internal assessment *must* play a large part in mathematical assessment.[8] Leaving a child's difficulties to be discovered at the end of the year would be like crying over spilt milk – and someone else would probably do the mopping-up! The ongoing programme is, therefore, of prime importance. Nevertheless, more formal procedures can be helpful. In choosing them, similar considerations are needed to those suggested for the use of internally produced tests.

1. Does the test cover what I need to assess?
2. Is it primarily computational, or does it test understanding?
3. Can it serve a diagnostic as well as attainment function?
4. Does it contain items which, for my children, would introduce irrelevant difficulties?
5. Is it going to add anything to my tools of testing? If so, what?

The NFER offers a wide range of mathematical tests, with different emphases in their construction. They fall into two main groups, the *Mathematics Attainment Tests,* and the *Basic Mathematics Tests.* Both titles may be initially misleading in suggesting an emphasis on computation. This is far from the case, as throughout there is an emphasis on understanding the operations involved, rather than on mechanical procedures. Test DE2, for instance, involves very little computation indeed (see Figure 8.1).

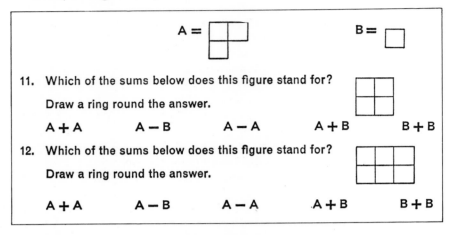

Figure 8.1   A test that emphasizes understanding. From *Mathematics Attainment Test*, DE2, NFER-Nelson.

The *Basic Mathematics Tests* were developed to provide material which would be relatively independent of details of teaching method, and thus bypass this source of inequality. Those for the primary range also provide a classification grid which categorises each question on a content-process grid. If this is completed for each child, it gives a profile of strengths and weaknesses which can be kept as a convenient record, both for individuals and the class as a whole. Such a method could, of course, also be used by teachers to classify the results of internally produced tests.

Whilst the NFER series are wide-ranging, they cannot be described as entirely coherent, either in terms of consistency of approach or of standardisation. Where a school desires a series which can be used throughout the junior stage, and which rests on a common standardisation basis, Young's 'Y' *Mathematics* may be helpful.

This has four overlapping stages, *Y1* to *Y4*. The first two of these have three sections: (a) orally presented items; (b) computation without the need for reading, and (c) written problems. The first two thus allow the poorer reader to show his achievements uncontaminated by reading problems. The later two stages have computation and written problem sections.

Young provides evidence of the stability of median scores across the four years of a junior school with an interval of one year between the administration of successive stages to the same group. Such consistency would be unlikely with the use of a less coordinated set of tests. The complementary *Group Mathematics Test* also provides oral and computational sections, principally for the top infant and first-year junior groups, but also applicable to less able pupils throughout the junior stage.

Another technique for avoiding the use of an assortment of tests is to choose one with a wide age range. Vernon again provides an example with his *Graded Arithmetic-Maths Test*. In his introduction to the revised edition, he points out the much greater heterogeneity of mathematics teaching in recent years, and the consequent problems for the test constructor. In his pilot studies, he found that some less traditional topics taught effectively in some classes were forgotten a year or so later. As he puts it, they were 'acquired parrot-like rather than forming a logical base for understanding more complex mathematical concepts' – the 'thin-ice' situation described earlier.

In contrast, traditional-type items showed a steady build-up without loss, and hence the test content is orientated towards traditional content. The manual gives quotients for the junior version from age 5.3 to 11.8, and suggested starting points in the test are given for different ages of pupil.

Screening and diagnosis

As suggested in the section on reading (see p.83), screening and diagnosis are often complementary functions – the screening procedure being used to indicate those in difficulties, the consequent diagnosis indicating the more precise nature of these difficulties. In mathematics, as in other areas, it is helpful if the two instruments work in tandem rather than derive from different sources.

This desirable situation is provided by the pairing of the *Basic Number Screening Test* with the *Basic Number Diagnostic Test*. Once more, in view of the variety of teaching approaches and content, it is the screening test that samples the basic number skills and concepts which most teachers are likely to expect children to know and understand – a 'common denominator' approach. It is presented orally, to avoid reading problems, and can be applied throughout the junior range. It gives 'number-age' norms (i.e., raw scores can be converted into number ages analogous with reading ages) and children scoring below a number age of 7½ can then be individually followed up with the diagnostic test. This is criterion- rather than norm-referenced, in that it 'seeks to show what a child can do (and cannot do) so that specific teaching objectives *for that individual child* can be determined'. The descriptive stage can thus lead on to the prescriptive. The content is again 'core' rather than wide-ranging.

As an aid to the setting of objectives within this core, a category grid is given on the front of the test form and it is suggested that, besides recording the present situation, an 'intention profile' should be shaded

Child's Name John Smith   Date completed 4. 9. 79

Date of Birth 25 · 8 · 73   Age 6 years   Number Age 5 years.

Categories	1—5	6—10	11—15	16—20	20+	Score
A1 Reciting numbers	▨	▨	▨			3
A2 Naming numbers	▨	▨				2
B1 Copying over	▨	▨				2
B2 Copying underneath	▨	▨				2
C1 Writing numbers in sequence	▨					1
C2 Writing numbers to dictation	▨					1
D1 Counting bricks	▨					1
D2 Selecting bricks	▨					1
E1 Addition sums with objects	▨					1
E2 Addition sums with numerals						
F1 Subtraction sums with objects						
F2 Subtraction sums with numerals						

Score ONE for each box ticked   TOTAL   14

Present attainments (shaded in)

Child's Name John Smith   Date completed ?. 12. 79.

Date of Birth 25 · 8 · 73   Age   Number Age

Categories	1—5	6—10	11—15	16—20	20+	Score
A1 Reciting numbers						
A2 Naming numbers						
B1 Copying over						
B2 Copying underneath						
C1 Writing numbers in sequence						
C2 Writing numbers to dictation						
D1 Counting bricks						
D2 Selecting bricks						
E1 Addition sums with objects						
E2 Addition sums with numerals						
F1 Subtraction sums with objects						
F2 Subtraction sums with numerals						

Score ONE for each box ticked   TOTAL

Objectives for three months' ahead (indicated by a dotted line)

Figure 8.2 A grid of attainment. From *Basic Number Diagnostic Test*, W.E.C. Gillham, Hodder and Stoughton, 1980.

in which indicates what is hoped to be achieved in three or six months time. Retesting will then indicate whether these objectives have been achieved (see Figure 8.2).

For those who are particularly interested in diagnosis within the mechanical aspects, Schonell's *Diagnostic Arithmetic Tests* (1957) and the associated *Diagnosis of Individual Difficulties in Arithmetic* provide food for thought, even though their original construction was before the Second World War.

The work of the APU

The NFER project *TAMS (Testing of Mathematical Attainment in Schools)* was already under way before the formation of the APU (see Chapter 1, p.10), and formed the basis of the APU monitoring programme.[9] The original intention was to assess the feasibility of a national survey of mathematics attainment using light sampling and item banking, providing a 'rolling' assessment in contrast to the use of a single measure at isolated points in time (as in the reading surveys from 1948 onwards). By 1982, three primary surveys had been carried out, the flexibility of the programme allowing different emphases in the balance of the survey programmes.

A particular feature of the work has been the inclusion of individual, practical testing. Thus, in the feasibility studies, items like the following were used:

Material	*Question*
15 marbles,	Give me $\frac{1}{3}$
Fine string, scissors, tape measure if requested	Cut off $\frac{1}{5}$

This type of item has been included throughout the subsequent APU surveys. Earlier work suggested that previous practical testing increased scores on later, comparable, written testing, but this has not always been the case. Comparison of orally presented items with comparable written ones has shown a lowering of performance on written as compared with oral items, with the effect strongest at lower levels of reading, as we would expect.

Besides these general effects on performance, examples were again found demonstrating the results of even slight variations in presentation. Thus from the third primary survey two parallel items (see Figure 8.3) showed startlingly different pass rates: 56% for D9 and only 26% for D11 with 20% omitting the item in this form.

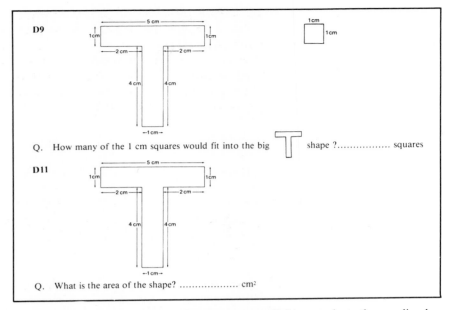

Figure 8.3   Comparison of responses to two parallel items where the wording has been altered. From the APU *Primary Mathematics Survey 3*.

Criticism has been expressed of the types of item used in the APU surveys, and fears expressed of backwash and Big Brother effects, but in these (as in all other APU surveys) anonymity of school and pupil is preserved, and the involvement of schools and pupils is minimal – only 1,000 schools and 13,500 pupils taking part in the third survey. The surveys, therefore, are far from being blanket operations.

The APU surveys of secondary mathematics have also thrown up occasional instances of 'regression in performance', with older pupils peforming less well than younger on comparable items. In commenting on similar findings from American surveys, it is suggested that 'the change is thought to be due to initial success based on operating a rule automatically, later overtaken by confusion as the child struggles to understand, with a subsequent improvement as understanding is achieved'.

This more sophisticated explanation nevertheless echoes Vernon's problem of the instability of some processes over time.

Notes

1   Guidelines are often constructed by panels of teachers, and published by the local authority. Is is well worth requesting copies from the local

authorities to gain a fresh look at the classification of mathematical objectives. E.g., Inner London Education Authority, *Curriculum Guidelines: Primary School Maths,* ILEA Publishing Centre.

Other well known guides are: Nuffield Foundation, *Guide to the Guides,* Chambers, 1973. This summarises the many individual guides available from this wide-ranging project.

Lister, J., *Notes on Guidelines in School Mathematics,* Hart-Davis, 1971, stems from the Mathematics Department of the Manchester College of Education.

2 Choat, E., *Mathematics and the Primary School Curriculum,* NFER, 1980.

The terms 'instrumental' and 'relational' understanding come from Skemp, R., *The Psychology of Learning Mathematics,* Penguin, 1971. Skemp is particularly against the 'blind' acquisition of mathematical knowledge.

3 Biggs, E., *Freedom to Learn,* Addison-Wesley, 1969. Schools' Council, *Mathematics in Primary Schools,* HMSO, 1969.

4 The example comes from Ward, M., *Mathematics and the Ten-Year-Old,* Evans, 1979. This account of a Schools' Council Project gives interesting data on what teachers thought was most important in mathematics and the relation between children's performance and those ratings. Those interested in following development towards the secondary school can consult Hart, K.M., *Children's Understanding of Mathematics,* John Murray, 1981.

5 *Check-ups:* Nuffield Foundation, *Checking-up I and II,* Chambers, 1970; Inner London Authority, *Checkpoints,* 1977.

6 Donaldson, M., *Children's Minds,* Fontana, 1978.

7 A simple introduction to item-banking is available from the NFER: Childs, R., *Item Banking,* NFER. This contains an account of the important Rasch model, which underpins much APU work. It aims at the production of items which are unaffected in difficulty by who is taking them, and which rank pupils in the same order whatever items are combined. It has, however, raised much opposition and controversy.

8 *Assessment:* Compared with the wealth of books on the testing of reading, there are few devoted to testing in mathematics. Possibly this is because the work itself is regarded as its own assessment. Useful suggestions can be found in Department of Education and Science, *Mathematics Counts,* (The Cockcroft Report), HMSO, 1982, Chapter 8. This report, whilst concerned with the teaching of mathematics in schools, sets the subject in a wide context, particularly in relation to the needs of adult life and employment. It also highlights mathematics as a form of communication.

Glenn, J.A., *Teaching Primary Mathematics,* Harper and Row, 1977, considers several taxonomies of objectives, and some very pertinent advice on the assessment of these.

9 The work of the APU: The APU had issued three reports on primary mathematics by the end of 1982. These are summarised in APU, Summary Reports, Nos. 1, 3 and 8, DES.

For further thought

1. What is your major purpose in teaching mathematics:
   - because it is useful in everyday life?
   - because it is a form of logical thinking?
   - because it is a form of knowledge that people can enjoy for its own sake?
   - because it is a form of education?
   - because it is an essential thread in other aspects of school work?
2. What do you understand by 'understanding' in mathematics?
   Are there some aspects that you would teach without requiring understanding because it is essential for children to 'get the answers right'?
3. What criteria would you adopt to satisfy yourself that your pupils knew the additive combinations of any two single-figure numbers?

9

The Assessment of Ability

The topic of ability, or *intelligence,* presents something of a dilemma: over the past 20 years or so, the trend has been against the testing of intelligence.[1] Few published tests now carry the term in their titles. American states have passed laws forbidding the use of IQ tests in their schools. Yet the everyday conversation of teachers is full of statements like 'He needs stretching', 'He doesn't seem to be working to his true potential', which indicate a belief in an 'intellectual horse-power' which may or may not be harnessed to the production of school work. This chapter will focus on the general arguments surrounding intelligence, rather than on specific tests since, whilst overt testing is on the decline, the attitudes of teachers towards the topic will be of fundamental importance in their assessment of their pupils.

What is intelligence?

The range of answers to this question is a wide one. For some, the concept has no value whatsoever. For others, it is a set of developed skills, as exemplified in the *Newsom Report's* belief that 'all children should be given the opportunity to acquire intelligence'. For Sir Cyril Burt, whose work made a profound impact on British educational thinking throughout the first half of the century, and indeed beyond, it was 'an *in-born,* all-round, intellectual ability'. Part of the confusion behind these views can be resolved by considering a simple classification proposed by Hebb (1966).

Hebb suggested that the term 'intelligence' could be used in two ways, which he called 'Intelligence A' and 'Intelligence B'. Intelligence A can be described as a 'genotype': a programme of development laid down at the outset – conception in humans, seed-production in plants. It is thus the genetic aspect of ability determined by the particular combination of genes derived from our parents. But the seed will not develop without soil, light and water, and the baby will not develop without an environment to nurture it.

Sometimes the environment will be an ideal one for the child, sometimes it will be unsuitable. In either case, the programme of Intelligence A will interact with the environment to produce Intelligence B – the programme in practice. This is the 'phenotype': the development we actually observe.

The phenotype may or may not completely reflect the genotype: we know from the Parable of the Sower that similar seeds placed in different soils suffer different fates – or, more technically, produce different phenotypes from the same genotype. Thus, we could argue, children of similiar Intelligence A could show different levels of 'everyday intelligence' (Intelligence B) if the environment of one was markedly beneficial to the development of the genetic programme, whereas that of another was inhibiting to development. An inanimate analogy would be to compare the performance of two equally high-powered cars – one running on its proper high-octane fuel, the other struggling along on two-stroke fuel. We would be wrong to say that the second car was worse than the first: it simply hadn't been given the appropriate nurturing.

So far, we have distinguished two usages of the term 'intelligence', the one (Intelligence B) perhaps closer to the Newsom notion of 'acquired' intelligence, the other to Burt's 'inborn' view. Vernon (1953) added a third, Intelligence C, which is very relevant to our concern with testing. Intelligence C is simply 'measured intelligence' – that is, the results achieved on an intelligence test. We cannot stay with a person all the time to monitor his 'Intelligence B', so we take a sample of it in the form of a half-hour or so of testing. The sample we take may or may not be the best from the pupil's viewpoint – in other words, it may or may not enable him to show his 'Intelligence B' to best advantage.

Can it be measured?

If we are talking about Intelligence C, then clearly the answer is 'Yes' since, by this definition, 'intelligence is what intelligence tests measure'. But if we accept that the particular test used gives only a sample, then different types of tests, offering different samples, might give different results. An obvious 'misfit' would be the administration of a written verbal test to a pupil with reading problems. A non-verbal test might well give a different, but *not,* as we shall see, a necessarily better result.

Not everyone, however, agrees that we are only getting at Intelligence C when using an ability test. Having defined intelligence as an 'inborn, general, intellectual ability', Burt concluded his statement thus: 'Fortunately it can be measured with accuracy and ease', thus creating, perhaps unwittingly, the impression that intelligence tests could give a measure of uncontaminated natural, inborn ability. Yet, at other times, he was at pains to point out that 'the results of the customary tests taken as they stand yield decidedly inaccurate estimates of potential ability when compared with the revised assessments reached after submitting the crude initial scores to the teachers and personally re-examining all doubtful cases'. How easy it is to slip from one usage to another, with subsequent confusion!

Cattell (1967) distinguished between two forms of intelligence: 'fluid', which is a kind of natural mental capacity which can be directed towards reasoning in any area of mental life, and 'crystallised' intelligence, which is the actual direction taken by this capacity as a result of the shaping influences of family, school and culture. 'Fluid' is thus similar to Intelligence A, and 'crystallised' to Intelligence B.

But tests can be heavily or only lightly saturated with knowledge acquired from a particular culture, and it may therefore be possible to find some which are more 'culture-fair' than others. Here is an item which is highly 'culture-bound':

Define the following:
    clarty   *galluses*   *dut*   *canches*

You can't? You're not very bright, are you? The answers, derived from Northumbrian culture, are: *muddy, braces, hat* and *pit-props*. A test derived from that culture would show quite clearly that Northumbrians are of superior intellect, fit to lead the rest of us, fit to take the superior positions and so on.

The parallel with black–white comparisons is painfully obvious, and has been pointed up by the *Black Intelligence Test of Cultural Homogeneity (BITCH)* which, being heavily loaded with specifically black cultural items, apparently demonstrates the superiority of blacks.

How, then could we get at a measure which was not culture-bound, which did not load the dice in favour of one cultural group rather than another? An example of a possible item is given in Figure 9.1. Its design is along the lines of Raven's *Progressive Matrices* and apparently (though you may like to think of possible objections) it is relatively culture-fair.

In interpreting the results of any ability test, we must therefore be clear whether we are treating them as a specific sample of mental life which may prove to be usefully related to future educational progress (e.g., in secondary or higher education, or in response to remedial provision); whether we are using them to rank individuals in terms of the 'learned skills' valued by a particular culture (Intelligence B, or

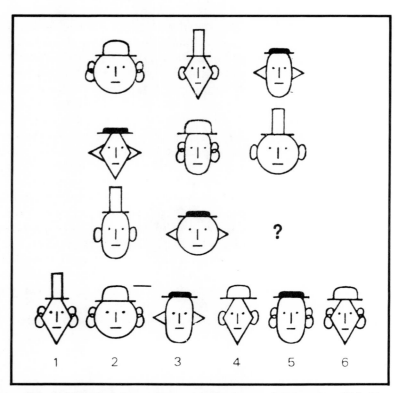

Figure 9.1   Which fits? From *Race, Intelligence and Education*, H.J. Eysenck, Temple Smith, 1971.

'crystallised' intelligence), or whether we think we have found a measure of pure natural ability, uncontaminated by cultural distortions (Intelligence A, or 'fluid' intelligence).

How are ability and attainment related?

If we take the Intelligence A view of intelligence, then we may feel that this represents, as suggested previously, a kind of intellectual horse-power which it is the teacher's task to harness. Children will be looked upon as having different capacities and the teacher's task will be to supply appropriate fuel, and tune the intellectual engine to its optimum performance. Other things being equal, she will expect the highest capacity to produce the highest performance, and she will probably feel that there is a limit to the performance for any given capacity. Crudely, you can't make a silk purse from a sow's ear.

This, indeed, is the 'capacity' view of intelligence, expressed by Burt (1937) as follows:

Capacity must obviously limit content. It is impossible for a pint jug to hold more than a pint of milk, and it is equally impossible for a child's educational attainments to rise higher than his educable capacity permits.

Three years later, Sir William Alexander (1940) spelt out the practical consequences:

Each child has his own standard, determined by his capacity. The task of the school is to educate each of its pupils in such a way that attainment is matched to capacity.

Those of us who began teaching in the 1950s were taught that the good teacher produced record cards where the attainment scores of pupils closely matched those derived from reasoning tests. As late as 1978, the State of North Carolina was reported to be publishing the results of five attainment tests in local newspapers together with the average IQ scores for each of its schools. So long as the subject score level was close to the IQ level, the school was regarded as doing a good job.

There are two major objections to this type of argument – the first general, and the second technical. The first again concerns the dangers of confusing different senses of intelligence: it may well be that our inbuilt 'computers' have different levels of full power. But to say that we have assessed this by particular tests is to risk an unwarranted jump from Intelligence C to A.

As an extreme example, before attention was paid to their plight, many spastics were labelled as ineducable since their speech was slurred, their movements uncoordinated, and they lacked normal means of communication. Yet, with eye-pointing and the use of feet rather than hands for writing, many have shown average or above-average abilities. Similarly Helen Keller, without Annie Sullivan's revealing teaching, would have remained a 'mute, inglorious Milton'.

The technical objection rests on work carried out with reading and non-verbal intelligence tests given to the same children. It was found that as many children 'over-achieved' (that is, performed better on reading than would have been predicted from their intelligence test score) as 'under-achieved'. Some children were working beyond their capacity, it would appear! In fact, the effect is inevitable if two tests have been standardised to a mean of 100 and the same spread. Unless there is perfect correlation between the tests (that is, unless they order the children in exactly the same way), some children *must* do better in Test A than in Test B, and some worse.

Whilst it is still possible to think of Intelligence A as a limiter of educational development, we thus cannot regard the results of an *actual* test as representing a ceiling of attainment. Rather, we should look on an ability measure as representing a sort of centre of gravity of likely educational performance: many children will indeed perform at about the level predicted, some will perform moderately higher or lower, and a few will perform very much higher or lower.

We thus have an actuarial prediction of the sort used by insurance companies. I might be told, at my advanced age, that I have only an expected further life span of 20 years – but this does not mean that 20 years is the limit of our expectancy, that we shall all die before then. Rather, it means that this will be the average expectancy, with some living a shorter period, and some, fortunately or not, living longer.

Teachers will no doubt be aware that the actual score on a test, whether of ability or attainment, can be raised by practice (allowing the child experience with similar items) or by coaching (giving specific teaching on the types of item in the test). But they should not imagine that they have increased the actual ability of the child by this help. What they have done is to raise the predicted level of attainment so that, in the heyday of the '11-plus', some heavily coached children entered grammar schools at the expense of uncoached children, since their raised scores suggested success in a grammar-type curriculum.

It was for this reason that 'practice for all' was suggested, with all pupils having a warm-up on the types of item to be encountered in the test proper. Thus, if a test has a practice section, it is most important that it is given in a proper way to the children. Equally, you *must* refrain from giving help beyond that which is recommended.

How are intelligence and personality related?

Whilst for some, intelligence is simply one aspect of the whole person, and therefore should not be divorced from personality, for others it has been an abstraction which can meaningfully be considered in its own right. Burt's 'all round, intellectual ability' was such an abstraction. He said it was 'intellectual, not emotional or moral, and remains uninfluenced by industry or zeal'.

Notice that Burt was talking about ability, and not the results of applying that ability. Although he was a strong supporter of the capacity view, he did admit that some individuals might 'over-achieve' and one reason he gave for this was 'an exceptional degree of industry'. We all know children whose ability seems to run to waste because of lack of persistence, distraction by outside influences and so on, whilst others of apparently less ability produce good results by relentless application. Michael Young summarised this in his book *The Rise of the Meritocracy* as an equation:

$$IQ + Effort = Merit$$

and Alexander had earlier suggested 'Factor X' which, besides including industriousness, combines those influences – parental encouragement, good teaching etc. – which can interact with ability to produce educational attainment.

Ability tests, then, do not directly measure such factors, but it is desirable to bear them in mind when interpreting results. Hence the importance of sound comments about personality factors when completing record cards.

Are intelligence and creativity the same?

Psychologists in America have tended to turn away from the idea of an all-round intellectual ability towards mapping a variety of differing abilities. The extreme position so far is that of Guilford, (1959) who has suggested no less than 120 possible facets of intellect. Included in these are the important operations of convergent and divergent thinking, the one concerned with 'homing in' on an already existing answer, as in

   Black is to *white* as *up* is to_____.

whilst the other is more open-ended, as in giving as many possible uses as possible for a brick, some of which will be conventional, mentioning some form of building, whilst others will be original and unexpected, such as 'To make a shallow jelly in'. This might then be described as a divergent response.

Whilst creativity should not be identified solely with divergent thinking, and divergent thinking should not be accepted as an activity for its own sake, Guilford contends very reasonably that the creative skills – revising the known, exploring the unknown – have perhaps not been given sufficient exercise in schools, and that this is not unconnected with the highly convergent nature of most intelligence and reasoning tests. Thus, it has been argued, we may be failing to identify important talent, and ignoring children of good, but different, potential.

Unfortunately, in spite of much research, tests which can adequately predict the emergence of specifically creative talent have not been forthcoming. But this does not mean that we should ignore the possibility of its existence. Hence the teacher should not allow her natural attention to the development of conventional abilities to blind her to other, less conventional, ways of being intelligent.

Is intelligence constant?

Once more, the answer to the question depends on what sense of intelligence we are using. The 'innate capacity' theory would suggest that Intelligence A determines the adult efficiency of the individual, granted the environment which is best suited to the development of his ability.

Burt said that 'we may safely assert... that the innate amount of potential ability with which a child is endowed at birth sets an upper limit to what he can possibly achieve both at school and in after-life'. But this once-off characteristic cannot, as we have seen, be directly measured, hence Vernon's forthright comment: 'Unfortunately it is not the slightest use to a psychologist since he has no means of observing, diagnosing and measuring it'.

We had, therefore, better confine ourselves to what can, in some sense, be measured – namely, Intelligence C. Here there are two aspects, the *absolute* and the *relative*. In absolute terms, the ability of the individual to develop new ways of thinking, as measured by the complexity of problems he can solve, appears to increase more and more slowly until it reaches a plateau, perhaps in the twenties, and thereafter tends to decline. Thus, surprisingly to some, the average 50-year-old is expected to score *less* on, say, the *Wechsler Adult Intelligence Test* than the average 20-year-old. In fact, he will have an age allowance in reverse!

In terms of relative standing, we can say quite definitely that individuals do not always retain their position relative to their peers. The general findings can be summarised as follows:

1. The earlier the testing, the poorer the prediction of final status. It would be very unwise to rely on pre-school testings alone as firm predictors of intellectual promise. For many, the indication will be reasonable, but for some the difference between estimate and outcome will be so great as to have devastating consequences were it acted upon.

2. The longer the interval between testings, the less accurate the prediction. The converse of this is, of course, that reliance on out-of-date testing (in attainment as well as ability) can give misleading results.

3. Different types of test will give different orderings of pupils. This follows from the fact that we are taking different samples when we apply different tests. Thus, a pupil's score on a non-verbal test may well differ from that on a verbal one, just as a pupil's reading score on words in isolation may well differ from that on comprehension questions following a connected passage. In a moment we shall turn to the important questions of whether one form of 'sampling' is fairer to the pupil than others.

4. No single test should be relied upon as a good predictor of future success. Put another way, the more reliable information we have, the

better our prediction is likely to be. For a whole variety of reasons – circumstances at the time of testing, the sample of skills offered to the pupil by the test, the fact that different children have differing growth rates in intelligence as in height – a score from a single test is not a label to hang on a child for the rest of his life.

5. Scores from individually administered tests of ability show greater stability than those from group tests administered by teachers.

So where do we stand?

On the utility of the concept of intelligence, Vernon (1979) stated his position thus:

> I do not see any particular value in retaining the term 'intelligence' as such, except that the general factor which runs through a wide variety of cognitive skills is too large to be ignored, and must be called something.[2]

But can we measure this important factor? Whilst he believes that there is no sharp distinction between ability and attainment tests, he agrees that the former involve more general skills of reasoning and comprehending which are widely applicable in educational situations, whilst the latter involve more specialised skills, depending more on the quality of school instruction.

The American, Jensen is more explicit and optimistic, however. In 1981 he wrote:

> No other item of information that we can obtain about a child will predict his verbal learning ability and academic achievement in school better than do scores on a recently administered IQ test. This is .... because they measure a general cognitive ability that plays a more important part in scholastic progress than any other trait.

How similar this is, after 50 years, to Burt's conclusion:

> Of all our mental qualities it is the most far-reaching: it is not limited to any particular kind of work, but enters into all we do or say or think.[3]

Implications for the teacher

If the teacher does use ability, reasoning or intelligence tests, the following cautionary notes should be borne in mind:

1. Tests do not give a clear indication of the uncontaminated natural ability of a child. Even the 'culture-fair' tests strongly advocated by Cattell show cultural effects.

2. Tests do not give an indication of the capacity of a child, if by this is meant a ceiling to his level of achievement. Rather, they suggest a broad band of possible achievement, the child's actual level being determined by other non-test factors such as persistence, encouragement and a possible bent by the child towards either the verbal-linguistic, or spatial-mechanical aspects of the curriculum.

3. Since the present primary curriculum is very much dominated by the written word and is strongly verbally biased, verbal tests are more likely to be predictive of educational success than non-verbal. Although non-verbal tests have been recommended in the past as fairer to non-readers, the NFER warns that their results should *not* be taken to indicate capacity for learning.

4. Different tests of ability are not equivalent: they present different samples, and are not alternative ways of getting at the same thing.

5. Single tests should never be used as a basis for important educational decisions.

6. Coaching and practice on any test beyond the limits suggested in the instructions are *not* beneficial to the long-term interests of the pupil.

7. It is important that children should have had adequate access to the content and conditions of the test used. Thus scores from 'test-naive' children (e.g., some immigrants) should not be taken as evidence of potential, and clearly the content should be reasonably familiar (cf. the *clarty* example on p.125).[4]

8. However, we should not indefinitely make allowances for lack of familiarity with content, etc. since immigrants, for instance, have to adapt and make their way in the culture which has produced the test, and not in their own original one.

External sources

Many verbal reasoning test agencies have dropped the title 'Intelligence' from their catalogues, replacing it by 'verbal (or non-verbal) reasoning'. The NFER describes its verbal reasoning tests as giving a 'measure of general scholastic ability. The results should *not* be taken to indicate capacity for learning'.

Readers are probably familiar with the types of item in such tests – analogies, similarities, opposites, codes, series, odd-man-out, etc. –

which are not directly part of the school curriculum but which test abilities which are important for success in a verbally-dominated educational system. They are less dependent, therefore, on fortuitous good or bad teaching than attainment tests. Indeed, it was for this reason that Godfrey Thomson began developing intelligence tests in the 1920s so that inequalities of educational provision should not prejudice children's chances of secondary education. Jensen (1981) writes:

> Mental tests by reading through the veneer of social class background can identify abilities wherever they occur, and thus may act as a leavening agent for the social mobility of able youngsters from lower SES backgrounds.

Non-verbal reasoning tests

These tests tend to be of two kinds: (1) picture tests for younger children, which present items similar to those of verbal reasoning tests in a pictorial form; and (2) tests which consist of abstract shapes, again echoing many of the types of item used in verbal tests. Because of 'contamination' problems, especially for poorer readers, the NFER suggest balancing verbal reasoning tests with non-verbal ones which avoid this problem.

The general consensus, however, is that verbal tests are the most effective predictors within a highly developed educational system. If a non-verbal test is to be used, then the arguments of Chapter 3 will still hold, in that a test such as Heim's *AH1*, which contains two parts, verbal and non-verbal, will be preferable to two separate tests from different stables.

Orally presented tests

A different way out of the contamination trap, without using a group non-verbal test, is to present the items orally, with the children selecting their response either by writing a number, or the initial of the answer they choose. Such a method avoids under-estimation because of reading difficulties.

Individual tests

A further method, not available to the ordinary teacher, is that of an individually-administered test. Until recently, when a child was referred to a school psychological service, it would have been fairly standard practice to administer either the *Terman-Merrill* test, or the *Wechsler Intelligence Scale for Children (WISC)*.[5] Vernon describes these as 'less biassed by such irrelevancies as facility in doing multiple-choice items at speed or comprehending printed directions' and as 'providing the most representative cross-section yet attained of daily-life cognitive schema over the age range'. It might seem from this that they are a better measure of Intelligence B than group-administered tests, but we still have to reckon with 'Factor X'. Teachers are often surprised by the performance of their pupils when given an individual test; whether scholastic results commensurate with the test occur depends on much more than the test itself.

Such tests can be useful when a teacher feels that a pupil has more to give than actually is produced in the classroom. An individual test can then provide a sound second opinion. The author was concerned at one time with a group of 'late-born' children (i.e. those born between May and August and thus lacking in a full infant stage). They were referred by the head teacher as possibly more able than their performance in basic work suggested. Individual testing confirmed this view in each case.

The use of such tests is, however, on the decline: psychologists are more and more turning to the investigation of the actual learning difficulty, and to the planning of programmes in consultation with the school, rather than the automatic administration of an 'intelligence' test. This again reflects the reduced importance of the concept of 'ability' in educational thinking.

The *British Intelligence Scale*, which has been a long while in production, has attempted to include some innovations in its construction. It has moved from the concept of a global figure, such as that given by the *Terman-Merrill*, to a profile approach (which is also provided by the *WISC*) and it has developed some very interesting material along Piagetian lines. It is as yet in the early stages of practical usage, but represents an attempt to produce a purpose-built test for British children, rather than adapt materials such as the *WISC* which originally were created in other countries.

Internal sources

The first point to be made is that teachers should *not* attempt the construction of reasoning tests. Their construction and interpretation are so clouded with difficulties that it simply is not worth the effort. Secondly, whilst teachers may feel that they can 'recognise ability' – and no doubt some can – the overall evidence is that the predictive validity of these efforts (as measured, for instance, by their correlation with attainment tests) is less than that of published tests. In other words, over a large number of pupils taught by a large number of teachers, equality is likely to be best served by the use of the same test, rather than by reliance on the varied 'judgeabilities' of the individual teachers.

It is obvious that the concept of intelligence, whilst apparently dead, is still kicking. It has political overtones, both within and between races: it is a sensitive area, since 'being intelligent' is still a kudos thing (witness MENSA) and, in the author's opinion, it still underpins many teachers' expectations of their pupils. Hence the need for teachers to assess what their own views are.

Notes

1   General accounts of the concept of intelligence can be obtained from any modern introductory text on educational psychology, such as Child, D., *Psychology and the Teacher,* Holt, Rinehart and Winston, 1977, Chapters 9 and 10.
2   Vernon, P.E., 'Intelligence Testing 1928–1978. What next?' SCRE, 1979, (or *British Journal of Educational Psychology,* 49, 1979), is a short and readable account of changes in thinking over half a century by one who has been closely concerned with the topic.
3   The controversial views of Arthur Jensen are powerfully presented in Jensen, A.R., *Straight Talk About Mental Tests,* Methuen, 1981.
4   A short account of the problems of possible unfair discrimination by tests is available from NFER; Pearn, M.A., *The Fair Use of Selection Tests,* NFER (note that 'selection' is used in a general, not a specifically educational, sense).
5   Accounts of the most commonly used individual tests can again be obtained from an introductory psychology text. The Terman-Merrill derives essentially from the work of Binet in France at the turn of the century, and hence has a long history.

Bibliography

Alexander, W.P., *The Educational Needs of Democracy,* University of London Press, 1940.
Burt, C., *How the Mind Works,* Allen and Unwin, 1933.
Burt, C., *The Backward Child,* University of London Press, 1937.
Cattell, R.B., 'The Theory of Fluid and Crystallised Intelligence', *British Journal of Educational Psychology,* Vol. 137, No. 2, 1967.
Guilford, J.P., 'Three Faces of Intellect', *American Psychologist,* Vol. 14, 1959.
Hebb, D.O., *A Textbook of Psychology,* Saunders, 1966.
Vernon, P.E., *Intelligence and Attainment Tests,* University of London Press, 1960.
Young, M., *The Rise of the Meritocracy,* Penguin, 1970.

For further thought

1. Do you see a place for the concept of 'intelligence' or ability in educational thinking? If so, what is your view of it?
2. Do you believe we have an upper limit or capacity to what we can do intellectually? Or do you think that, given time and the right circumstances, anyone can learn anything?
3. Have you met any 'late developers'? To what would you ascribe their blossoming?
4. Can you recognise ability when you see it? If so, what are the signs? What evidence have you that you were right in your judgements?
5. Do you use any reasoning, ability or intelligence tests in your school? If so, for what purposes? Do they satisfy these purposes?
6. Is 'intelligence' just one facet of personality to you, or do you see it as something different?
7. Do you think children can learn to be intelligent? If so, how?
8. Have you any views on the nature-nurture, heredity-environment argument? If so, do they affect your teaching?

10

Reporting and Recording Assessment

In this final chapter there will be an opportunity to review the arguments of previous chapters by considering how different kinds of information – internal, external, observational, formal – can be gathered together to best advantage. It may be wise to recall that the title of this book, *Testing for Teaching,* implies that tests or other assessment procedures are the servant of the teacher, not the master. There is a break-even point in record-keeping beyond which time and energy are being taken away from the task of teaching without any extra benefit accruing either for teacher or pupils. Rather rudely, one might say that 'weighing the pig won't fatten it'.

Some general principles reapplied

Objectives

With economy of time and effort as our guides then, we can look once more at objectives, though in a slightly different way. Instead of asking, 'What are our objectives in *teaching*?' we can ask, 'What are our objectives in *recording*? Who is going to be helped by it, and how?' Here we can distinguish several possible beneficiaries:

The teacher herself. Both *formative* and *summative* information will be of value. Ongoing records of work done, progress made, attitudes and behaviour will guide the planning of future work (the formative aspect) and, gathered together, will form a basis for a final summation at the end of the year, probably presented in a more standardised and permanent form than the 'internal' records of the teacher herself.

Other teachers in the school. In the primary school, where children remain, by and large, with the same teacher for a year, summaries from the previous teacher of work done and standards achieved by both the class as a whole and by individual pupils will obviously be of value in planning the future year's work. There will, however, also be occasions, such as illness, requiring the use of a supply teacher when it is important that the class teacher's ongoing record is adequate to get her temporary replacement started in the right direction.

Teachers in other schools. Two situations exist here. In one, which might be called *transition,* all children move together from one stage of education to another – from infant to junior to secondary school. Many authorities, of course, have a standardised card or booklet on which the summative evaluation of the completed stage is recorded. But, as we shall see, the existence of a standardised form is no guarantee that the information on it is standardised. The need for some uniformity is of course greatest when children from several 'feeder' schools enter a new stage of education together.[1]

The second 'movement' situation, *transfer,* occurs when a child moves individually from school to school – most frequently because of a change of address. Again, the new school needs concise, readily interpreted and accurate information to help settle the newcomer effectively. Where, as in Britain, there is great variety of curriculum practice, there is an equally great responsibility on the 'sending' school to be as helpful as possible.

Interested parties outside the school system. For the primary school, parents will be the most frequent 'receivers' outside the school. Usually, these will be lay observers, and thus the school has the difficult task of translating onto a short report form the distillation of a year's work. Since the majority of parents will not have the technical background of teachers, it is important that communication is clear and unambiguous, so that reports are fair both to all the children of a particular class, and between the classes of a particular school.

The pupils themselves. The pupil's own work is a kind of record of its own: a mathematics book shows, at least in 'product' terms, what has been done and achieved, and some schemes, such as the SRA laboratories, carry their own built-in record. Schools can take this further by having their pupils record, for instance, books that have been read, work done in projects, creative work and so on. This ensures a wider coverage of pupil performance than a busy teacher could manage on her own – but taken from the viewpoint of the pupil.

There is no reason why such pupil records, together with the teacher's own records, should not form the basis of feedback to the pupil: 'You're getting really interested in reading now: what a change from the beginning of the year!' Pupils are, after all, 'interested parties' too!

Consistency

Whilst a teacher may be able to interpret her own records consistently, the outline above shows that they will also be transmitted to others. In such a transfer, consistency is all-important if misunderstandings are to be avoided.

Internal measures

Two kinds of consistency are needed here: self-consistency and consistency between teachers. In the primary school, a single teacher reports on a variety of pupils in a variety of situations. It is important, therefore, that there is consistency in reporting standards for different pupils, and that these are made clear to those who see the records or reports.

We have seen in Chapter 5 how consistency can be aimed at in acquiring information: it would be a pity to lose this by inconsistency in reporting. Much inconsistency can be avoided by making clear what is reported on, and what the reference group is. Thus, on a report, the comment 'Good progress made this year in reading, although he needs to read more carefully if he is to reach the average level for his age' is different from: 'A good term's work. Below average'. In the first, the two reference points – for *progress*, the child's initial status, and for *attainment*, an average level (but which?) – are indicated. Without reference points, misinterpretations can occur.

Similar problems affect comparisons between children from different classes. Suppose two teachers in the same school teach different classes of the same age. In preparing their record cards or reports they decide to use a five-point scale to record standards: apparently we have a common scale. But if the two teachers are working to a different central point (i.e. what they consider average) and to different spreads of scale, comparisons between the children of the two classes will be distorted.

Differences in the reference points can occur through personal experience ('Oh dear, this lot's not a patch on most of the third years I've had' in which case there will be a distortion or 'skew' to the lower end of the scale). The gloomy parents of Miss A's children will receive a high proportion of 'below average' comments on their reports, whereas the reports of Miss B (who has just moved from five years' remedial teaching) will delight parents with the enthusiasm of the grading. (See Figure 10.1).

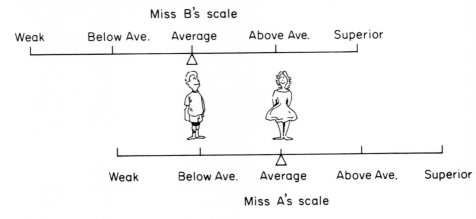

Figure 10.1   Different teachers, different ratings. Mary is Above Average for Miss B, but only Average for Miss A. Jack is Average for Miss B, but Below Average for Miss A.

Even where the performance of the class itself is taken as the reference point, there can be problems. Suppose that, objectively speaking, Miss A's class have an overall standard which is much higher than Miss B's. If both use their own class average as a standard, some children who receive an average rating by Miss A would have received an above average rating by Miss B. Thus, where comparisons outside the class are needed, or implied, a common reference point is needed. Reports to parents, orders of merit where selective procedures are still in operation, transition records for secondary schools – all these, for fairness, require the existence of a common reference point.

One can talk glibly of setting a standard or reference point for a year group, but in the primary school, this may not be easy. There is not, as in a secondary school, the opportunity for comparing notes with other teachers who meet our children, and by and large the class teacher is thus the main arbiter of standards of internal assessment. How, therefore, can overall standards be set?

One possibility would be to supplement the 'private' judgement of the teacher with a more 'public' judgement by, say, a published test. If an objective measure – a reading or number test, as appropriate – which is valid and applicable to the curriculum of the school is used, then the values of the first-hand experience and impressions of the teacher can be combined with the more impersonal values of the test.

Such a test can then be used to 'calibrate' the subjective opinions of teachers: as a crude example, if Miss A, whose children have an average reading score of 107, describes many of her children as 'below average' whilst Miss B, whose class achieves an average of 97, has many of her group as 'above average', then it is likely that two different standards are operating.

With transition records, the situation is more complex. We not only have the possibility of different teachers operating different standards, but of different schools having different general reference points, so that Uptown's geese are indubitably Downtown's swans. The arguments given above can be used to support authority-wide testing – but in no sense should this be used to dominate the year-long observation of the teacher: far better for teachers to move towards a common standard by discussion amongst themselves, than to have it imposed on them by 'blanket testing'.

Another external, though not completely objective, source of comparison is the Head teacher. Monitoring of performance by the Head can serve a variety of assessment purposes, both for teachers and pupils, provided it is done in an atmosphere of cooperation, and not as Big Brother or Sister looking in. By a sampling of children's work on a rota system – say a week's output from four children from each class per month – the Head can develop a feel for the general quality of work in the school, the standards operating in different classes, and the progress of different pupils. When any question of comparative standards becomes important, the Head can act as a stable reference point.

Such a system can also provide feedback to the pupils, either directly or through the teacher, so that they feel that Sir or Madam is an involved and not a remote figure. Similar advantages will also occur when the Head teaches different classes in the school.

External measures

The advantage of greater consistency has been given above as a reason for reporting results on an external test. But even so, care must be taken in using the results of such tests. To summarise the arguments of Chapter 4, it is desirable to aim for tests which:

– are standardised to a consistent mean and standard deviation or spread (usually 100 and 15 for modern tests);

– have high reliabilities (since this reduces the standard error of measurement);

– have been well standardised;

– have as much relevance as possible to the work of *all* the children who will be taking them: otherwise some will be at a disadvantage when compared with others.

In the interpretation of such tests, it is also important to aim for consistency: there is little point in going to the expense and trouble of buying tests as an objective standard if teachers use varying interpretations of scores in their reports. It would be unfortunate if two children in separate classes, each scoring 115, were labelled as 'good average' and 'above average' respectively from the results of their tests. Where would objectivity be then?

The content of records and reports

Since this book is about testing, not all features which could usefully figure in records will be considered here. References for the development of overall plans of records-keeping are given at the end of this chapter.[2]

Types of record

The analysis given above can be reduced to two major types, those of *contemporary* and *consecutive* reporting. The contemporary type is an ongoing record, which in the primary school will be used and developed mainly by the class teacher. It may include a variety of evidence: a general diary of events which can be reviewed when summary information is needed; a page-by-page record for each child, perhaps with a format which the teacher has found useful; records and checklists of work done and skills achieved or not achieved; results of tests, displayed both for the class and for individual pupils.

Reliance on a standardised form is not desirable at this stage, since teachers may try to carry observations in their head, hurriedly hunting through their memories when it is time for the cards to be completed. A standardised form may also restrict the flexibility of an individual teacher's recording of data useful to her.

Checklists (see p.63) are obviously useful in ensuring that the teacher is systematic in her observations within a particular area. They can, however, be extremely detailed, particularly at the early stages, and care should be taken to select or develop those which provide the essential information with minimum disruption of normal classroom work. Thus, checks which can be carried out whilst the child is engaged on his usual activities are preferable to those which require special test materials and a test-like atmosphere.

In completing a checklist, it is important to be clear how success or failure is to be recorded. What does a tick mean? That he shows absolute proficiency in the skill? That he can 'just about manage it'? Criteria which are as clear as possible should be established –

otherwise there will again be inconsistency in checking the activities of different children. An alternative is to use, say, a four-point scale as indicated in Figure 10.2. Here, degrees of proficiency can be indicated, together with dates which will show how progress is being made.

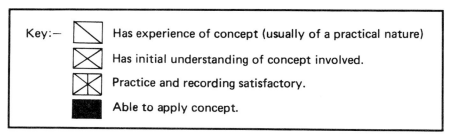

Figure 10.2   Degrees of proficiency; a rating scale from the Wiltshire County Council's 'Record and Transfer Document in Mathematics'.

In summary then, the contemporary record might include:

1. A diary, perhaps on a weekly basis. This should not be of the 'stream of consciousness' variety in which things just float to the surface of the teacher's mind, but should have some structure, as indicated in Chapter 5.

2. Records of class tests. The name of the test, and date given, *must* be recorded. It is not sufficient to head the page 'Reading test results' because (a) other teachers may unwittingly give the same test when they receive the children; (b) dating enables progress to be more clearly seen; and (c) the type of test – e.g., in reading, word recognition, comprehension, etc. – may be important.

3. Graphical displays. Simple histograms can give 'at a glance' information of value as: (a) baseline data, as in the allocation of children to reading groups and in the allocation of appropriate books to children; (b) consecutive data, gives their next teacher a quick summary of, for instance, the results of tests used at the end of a year; (c) progress data, e.g. by superposition of histograms of testing done at the beginning and end of the school year.

Some general points of balance

The 'instrumental' aspects of school life (knowledge, skills etc.) are easier to observe and record than the 'expressive' (the values, attitudes of pupils). But both, of course, are important. Therefore an appropriate balance should be aimed at in recording and reporting. It is important to know that John has shown persistence in his reading, in spite of a low average attainment, whereas Alex is 'coasting' in spite of a high level of attainment. Considerations of balance will also lead the teacher to comment on Silent Sally in the corner as well as Extrovert Eric, whom nobody could miss, and who might thus carry more than his fair share of (probably adverse) comment. Some suggestions for achieving balance in the observation of pupils were given in Chapter 5.

This then leads to the question of how much 'trouble' should be recorded, and how much success. Some writers suggest that trouble needs more attention than the 'set fair' situation, and certainly the *1981 Schools Council survey of record-keeping* showed that trouble factors – referral to outside agencies, to psychological services, to remedial agencies – were high on the list of priorities for recording. The argument is logical enough: a simple tick or positive statement showing that the expected has been achieved may be sufficient for those progressing normally, but further investigation and diagnosis is needed when things are not as expected.

Within the more strictly academic parts of the curriculum it is important that, even if specific records are not kept separately for history, geography and science (since frequently these are treated by means of topics or projects) some account is taken of the work in reporting on pupils. Her Majesty's Inspectors found science particularly poorly represented in the curriculum of the primary school.[3]

One problem, of course, is the flexibility of the topic approach. As the Schools Council report, *Evaluation, Assessment and Record-Keeping in History, Geography and Social Sciences*, says: 'Every teaching situation is unique, according to the unique blend of teacher, school, children and environment concerned'. Some suggestions for science record-keeping can be obtained from Harlen (1977).

In the assessment of project work itself, teachers have generally admitted that presentation is a major factor in their appraisal. There are, however, several other important skills which can be judged from the children's efforts. In particular, the development and use of study skills can be noted and recorded as suggested on pp.142–43. The project situation is a far more realistic one for the exercise of these skills than more deliberate exercises. It is salutary but sad that in the Schools' Council report, study skills such as use of an index took extremely low positions (from 101 downwards!) in teachers' ratings of their importance in recording.

Teachers cannot have it both ways: if they react against the assessment of knowledge gained from project work on the grounds that the children should be learning how to learn, then some means of assessing whether they are indeed doing so should be provided.

General problems of records and reports

Availability
Teachers vary in the extent to which they wish to consult record cards for their children. Some, mindful of 'expectation effects', prefer not to look at them too early. Others feel the need for guidance from previous teachers. For similar reasons, some schools keep records separately, not consulted by teachers until the time for completion again comes round. Again, the argument is that each teacher should report on a 'clean sheet' basis. This may apply particularly to comments on personality and attitudes.

Scope
How much should be recorded is an important issue. To some extent, this depends on the length of time the record covers. The *Wiltshire Record and Transfer Document in Mathematics*, covering the years 5–13, has a total of 171 checks to be recorded on a four-point scale. This seems an enormous task, until it is realised that eight years are available, and that much of the recording will result from the teacher's day-to-day work rather than from massive intrusions on her time.

A 'cumulative' record of this sort, which provides in one document an effective source of ongoing, baseline and summative data can thus be more economical than might at first seem. A parsimonious rule to adopt might be: 'Collect enough information for the purpose required, *and no more*'.

Personality
It must be admitted that, in spite of the lip service given to the development of personality by schools (and no doubt many do attempt this), singularly little external material is available for its assessment, so that the teacher may be thrown onto her own resources. The subjectivity of these can be so great that it has been said that statements about pupils reveal more about the attitudes of the rater than they do about the pupil.

Personality as revealed by behaviour can be very situation-specific: John persists with his number work, but is uninvolved in his reading. Mary gets along fine with Miss A but spits fire with Mr. B. Jack is docile at school, but a devil at home. Such variations are part of everyday life outside school, and teachers must report on the realities of their interactions with their pupils, not on some abstraction which might be the 'real' pupil. But, to avoid unnecessary inconsistency, some common points are essential to avoid this sombre comment by Vernon:

> The ratings given on record cards by primary school teachers from numerous different schools are of practically no value to the secondary

school teacher of the same pupils, because the latter cannot know what different distributions the different raters adopted.[4].

The common points are:

1. Try to standardise the vocabulary of rating. Many of the terms used in rating personality are in common use and can imply different things to different people. Thus, one study of the meanings of the term 'reliability' showed two major divisions: those teachers for whom it meant relatively placid and submissive behaviour ('He can be relied on not to make trouble!') and others for whom it meant a more active behaviour, including initiative. Thus the use of a common term does not necessarily mean that a common trait is being rated.

2. Any trait should be rated across several aspects of school life. Persistence, for instance, may vary with the situation – good in learning a new motor skill, poor in linguistic work. If one teacher has a different 'scan' when considering persistence, she will not have a common basis with others for her ratings. Thus a set of suggestions for situations will be helpful in preventing too narrow a spread of situations.

3. It is generally held that rating of each trait for a class is preferable to rating each individual as a whole on all the traits. In others words, persistence is looked at across the class, then reliability, and so on. This avoids the halo effect, and helps to ensure that a spread of rating occurs in each trait.

4. A common scale is desirable, preferably of the graphic variety as shown in Figure 10.3. The rater simply puts a mark at the most appropriate point on the line.

Needs much prodding in doing ordinary assignments	Needs occasional prodding	Does ordinary assignments of his own accord	Completes suggested supplementary work	Seeks and sets for himself additional tasks

Figure 10.3   A common scale. From *Personality Tests and Assessments*, P.E. Vernon, Methuen, 1953.

5. Many teachers will no doubt think that breaking down personality into subdivisions is unreal, and therefore some use a thumb-nail sketch system, where a set of guidelines is given which the teacher uses to frame the sketch. Thus, one authority guide contains the following:

Character: Include comments on: helpfulness/cooperation/leader-ship/reliability. Does he need constant reassurance/supervision, or is he self-disciplined? Does he show enthusiasm, determination, etc.? Does he respond to encouragement/resent criticism?

Whilst this avoids the breakdown of individual rating of traits and gives all teachers a similar guide, it still can be ambiguous, as we have seen, because of different interpretations of vocabulary, and biases in observation.

To summarise the major part of this chapter, we can say that consistency must always be aimed at, both in the use of formal procedures and in the informal and vital daily interchanges between teacher and pupil.

Notes

1 For an account of a project involving teachers which was specifically designed to improve assessment procedures at transition from junior to secondary school see Sumner, R. and Bradley, K., *Assessment for Transition*, NFER, 1977. The materials arising from the project are available as 'Transitional Assessment Modules', ten for mathematics and eight for English, covering different types of essay writing, cloze and comprehension passages, and 'surface' measures.
2 Clift, P., *Record Keeping in Primary Schools*, Schools' Council, 1981; Cooper, K., *Evaluation, Record Keeping and Assessment in History, Geography and Social Science*, Collins, 1977; Harlen, W., *Match and Mismatch*, Oliver and Boyd, 1977; Rance, P., *Record Keeping in the Progressive Primary School*, Ward Lock, 1972; Shipman, M., *In-School Evaluation*, Heinemann, 1979.
   A down-to-earth and brief examination of records is given by: Frisby, C., 'Records and Assessment', *Forum*, 1982, Vol. 24, No. 2.
3 DES, *Primary Education in England*, HMSO, 1978, pp. 58–63. Chapter 4 gives some general information on records.
4 Vernon, P.E., *Personality Tests and Assessments*, Methuen, 1953, Chapter 7.

For further thought

1. When taking over a new class, do you like to look at previous information early on, or do you leave it until you have got to know the class?

For group discussion

1. What attitudes are there in the group towards reports? Do some schools not use them at all? Do some make them available on request? Do some have a standard form? Do some prefer to report orally rather than in a written form?
2. Where standard forms are used, compare these for their content (e.g., emphasis on 'instrumental' and 'expressive' aspects of school life); for the use of scales, either literal or numerical; and for their ability to present an adequate account of a year's work and behaviour.
3. Bring along and discuss some of the following:
   – checklists in reading and mathematics,
   – examples of 'ongoing' recording (e.g. diaries),
   – records completed by pupils themselves (e.g., books read, assignments completed).
4. Which children in your class do you know least about? Why? Which children in your class do you know most about? Why? In which subjects do you have most knowledge of your pupils' performance? in which least?